Angela -
an in
this was quite an experience!

LIFELINE TO A SOUL

THE LIFE-CHANGING PERSPECTIVE I GAINED WHILE TEACHING ENTREPRENEURSHIP TO PRISONERS

We all deserve second chances -
it's how we learn.

JOHN K. McLAUGHLIN

Lifeline Education Connection
Charlotte, North Carolina

Lifeline to a Soul: The Life-Changing Perspective I Gained While Teaching Entrepreneurship to Prisoners

Published by Lifeline Education Connection,
Charlotte, North Carolina

LIFELINE
EDUCATION CONNECTION

ISBN 979-8-9866891-0-4 (paperback)
ISBN 979-8-9866891-1-1 (eBook)
Library of Congress Control Number: 2022917199

www.Lifelinetoasoul.com.

The stories in this book reflect the author's recollection of events. Some names, locations, and identifying characteristics have been changed to protect the privacy of those depicted. Dialogue has been re-created from memory.

Publication managed by AuthorImprints.com

To anyone who has broken the law, learned from the experience, and became a better person because of it.

Table of Contents

Foreword

WE'RE ALL ABOUT THE SAME. Great men find themselves often tested, and for good reason. I don't know if I knew I was being tested in the moment. I probably would have come up with some sort of excuse as to why I was there and how I got myself into that situation. I look back and laugh these days; I laugh at past failures while enjoying today's success. I wonder what I would have been if I had known my natural inclination toward risk-taking and the unknown were high-value qualities found in all great men. I wonder if I had met a guy like John earlier in my life, and had been inspired by his work and success, maybe I'd have seen things differently. You only know what you've seen, we dream of a life far away but your experiences and influences are what make you, you.

This book is about a man who took the time to separate himself from the notions of others, and set out to find the truth. Prisons are dark, scary places to most and John will tell you he had no clue what he was getting into. But that's where the separation lies—he still took the risk. He went in with an open mind with only the desire to teach and as a result, learn. Real knowledge, real experience, and real insight is what John brings to the table. A tried-and-true business owner meets hardened criminals, with one intention: find common ground and break free. I hope this book finds you in good spirits and that you can read it openly. That you can enjoy the humor, that you can feel the fear at times, and most of all that you learn something from a guy who's quite literally, seen it all.

Omar Markabi
September 2022

Prologue

I KNEW PRISON WAS IN my future.

Here I was, twenty-one years old, standing in the dining room of the restaurant where I waited tables while my manager and two uniformed police officers detailed their knowledge of an illegal drug trade operating on the property and their intention to fix it. In the trunk of my car was half a pound of marijuana.

That the impromptu meeting was taking place on the same night as my biggest potential drug deal could not be a coincidence. They knew. They had to.

I recently left Western Illinois University and enrolled at the University of North Carolina at Charlotte (UNCC). I had very little cash saved and planned on taking a year off from college to make some money. I landed a job waiting tables, and the manager—the same one staring me down—had taken an interest in me. He wanted to make me an assistant manager and teach me how to properly run a restaurant.

"Seems like a lot of hours for not much money," I told him, with the type of unearned arrogance reserved exclusively for twenty-one-year-olds.

I'd found another way to make money, anyway. Shortly after I'd arrived in Charlotte, I learned that someone I looked up to was an active drug dealer. I soon began helping out with the side business and was able to find a ready supply of marijuana customers among the staff at the restaurant. As word grew that I had quality product, the dime bag sales became half ounces, and before long, full ounces. As the sales volume increased, our supplier had an opportunity to make a big buy of some high-quality weed and asked if we'd be interested in buying a full pound. My cohort and I decided the best way to capitalize on the opportunity was to presell half of the pound, which would pay for most of the other half and wouldn't strain our cash flow.

I asked around the restaurant and found a coworker who was interested in buying the half-pound but wanted to inspect it first. I agreed to bring the drugs to work and leave them in the trunk of my car. The plan was to give him my car keys during break so that he could view the goods. If the product met his expectations, he'd grab it and leave the money in the trunk of my car. It should've been seamless, but my prospect called off the deal when he returned from the inspection.

"Too much shake" is all he'd said. Unbeknownst to me, my literal partner in crime had gone through the half-pound I'd planned to sell and removed all the choice buds, which produced the best high. It put me in the unfortunate predicament of having a substantial amount of marijuana in the trunk of my car and two uniformed officers standing in front of me who looked to be very aware of it . . . and also very ready to take me to jail.

"We've been watching the parking lot for a few weeks now, and we think we know who's involved," my manager explained confidently, snapping me back to reality.

I was sure the police were going to make me open the trunk of my car, confiscate the drugs, and take me directly to jail. Possession of over an ounce and a half of marijuana carried a twenty-five- to thirty-month prison sentence, and all my assets in the world amounted to less than $500. I'd have to hire a public defender, plead guilty, and do time. All I could think about was how disappointed my parents were going to be.

I was so mentally mired in despair that I didn't realize the speech was over and the dining room had almost emptied. Remaining there would look suspicious, but the room felt safe, and I lingered. That would be my last oasis of normalcy for some time.

When I could stay there no longer, I drew a long, shaky breath and grudgingly walked toward my fate.

CHAPTER ONE

All Things Come to Those Who Wait

"If somebody offers you an amazing opportunity but you are not sure you can do it, say yes—then learn how to do it later!"

—Richard Branson, British business magnate

AS I DROVE TO THE prison through rural North Carolina communities and past fragrant, budding fields on a warm spring morning, I prayed a silent prayer of thankfulness for the opportunity that had *finally* presented itself. I was on my way to a job interview about an hour away from my home in Charlotte. If hired, I'd have a position teaching a community college course on entrepreneurship.

Thankful the GPS app was guiding my progress, I sat alone at a desolate intersection next to a white clapboard Baptist church. While waiting for the app to confirm I was on the right path, I noticed the church's sign appropriately read, "God's help is only a prayer away." My trip to the interview was almost complete, but it was a journey that started long ago.

Eight years prior, I knew I wanted to become an adjunct business instructor. Since then, I'd spent several thousand dollars on more than thirty credit hours of graduate-level college work to get my resume in shape. I sent hundreds of resumes, applied to numerous colleges who advertised adjunct teaching positions, and presented as a guest speaker to local community colleges in hopes of convincing someone I could teach somebody something. My last birthday put me closer to fifty-five than fifty, and I realized my advancing age combined with my lack of teaching experience probably explained the disinterest.

Undeterred, I pressed forward and hoped for a break. The upcoming interview was the sum of all my efforts—my first in-person instructor interview—and it felt great that I'd convinced a learning institution of any stripe that I was qualified to teach. Or, at the very least, that I was worthy of an interview. Because getting the meeting had taken eight years of effort and I wasn't getting any younger, I surmised that my window of opportunity in the teaching field was closing quickly. I was determined to give it my best shot.

My interview was to take place in a minimum-security prison, which was also where I'd be teaching if everything went the way I hoped. I'd never set foot inside a prison before but was so eager to teach that I was willing to overlook where it would take place, be it inside a prison fence or on the surface of the moon. As I passed a hand-painted "Eggs for Sale" sign posted at the end of a long gravel driveway, I followed the app's last instruction and turned right on Palisade Prison Road. Thinking back to the unforeseen series of life events that led me there, I figured that I probably wasn't the first guy traveling down Palisade Prison Road who'd reflected on his past and the decisions that had led him to that destination.

I arrived at the prison twenty minutes early, providing me with an opportunity to size the place up. A weary-looking chain-link fence with a few thin strands of sagging barbed wire between the top of each post encircled the camp. A large gravel parking lot full of pickup trucks and sedans bordered the east fence. There were three aging school buses painted off-white with metal bars covering the windows and *NC Department of Corrections* painted on the sides. A chain-link gate big enough to drive a truck through separated the gravel lot from the prison yard. Deep tire tracks in the soft earth had created a large gap between the bottom of the sagging gate and the ground.

I could crawl under that if I wanted to.

The prison consisted of three squatty old brick buildings toward the front, a large modular building in the far front corner, and a tiny, prefabricated aluminum guardhouse that sat on a small, raised platform front and center, bridging the boundary between freedom and incarceration. Directly before the small guardhouse was a paved lot with reserved parking signs and a fleet of white Chevrolet Malibus with state decals on the doors and government-issued license plates. Inside the fence was what appeared to be a homemade wooden carport with stacks of free weights and semi-rusted weight-lifting equipment underneath. A huge man with dreadlocks was rapidly bench-pressing what I estimated to be at least three hundred pounds while his spotter urged him on.

The prison yard appeared to be extremely well-kept. Ventilated plastic benches were anchored into slabs of concrete with patches of deep blue and yellow wildflowers growing on each side-beauty blooming in the grit. A medium-sized speckled hound napped near a large yucca plant that was strategically placed next to a concrete Ping-Pong table whose net was patched with silver duct tape. Men wearing matching heather-gray T-shirts and army-green pants stood in an unorderly line in front of a tan brick building with a sliding counter-height window. The feature attraction of the small prison yard seemed to be a full-size concrete basketball court, where six men played a half-court game of three-on-three.

Since it was my first time at any prison, I was unsure how to gain entrance but figured the tiny guardhouse would be a good place to start. I parked in an open space in the paved lot, noticing a well-dressed blond woman emerging from her car. It was Sarah, the director of business training from the community college and the person who'd arranged my interview.

Sarah directed me to follow her in my car to the right side of the prison, where a small oblong building stood behind a chain-link fence with a gate that had a substantial-looking padlock through its hasp. Just outside the fence was a two-acre plot of land being prepared to plant some sort of crops. When we arrived at the gate, Sarah instructed me to leave my phone in the car—phones weren't allowed inside the prison. We waited until a fit-looking man with a long gray ponytail exited the building, walked down the concrete steps, and unlocked the gate for us. He introduced himself as Richard.

Richard was small-town Southern friendly, and he kindly ushered us up the steps into the programs office. Sarah and I followed as he led us through the dimly lit building, explaining that we would be meeting in the prison chapel's conference room. Richard produced a wad of keys from his pants pocket and unlocked the program's office door, waited for us to enter the building, and closed and locked the door behind us. He obviously knew his way around the prison and opened every door and gate we needed to walk through, carefully locking everything behind us until we arrived at our destination. The conference room, I later learned, was sometimes called the "side pocket." It was a small rectangular room directly inside the front door of the chapel and contained a conference table so large that we could barely pull our chairs out without hitting the walls.

My interviewers were Sarah; Richard, who taught the commercial cleaning part of the class; and another man, Frank, who was waiting for us in the conference room.

The program offered by the college was designed to assist those who were likely to have trouble finding a job upon their release from prison since they would have a felony on their record. The subject matter combination of cleaning and entrepreneurship made a lot of sense to me. Starting a business was a great option for those struggling to find work due to a prison record, and what better business to start than a cleaning business, which has low start-up costs and a huge potential market?

Frank Kemper was the man in charge of enrolling students and making sure the classes ran properly. He was a bald, stocky, forty-something man who wore a disturbed, quizzical look on his face and spoke with a lazy Southern accent. With his body build, bald head, and annoyed look, he resembled a pissed-off Mr. Clean. The three interviewers sat together on one side of the oversized table and shared an inside joke about whose turn it was to make coffee. It was obvious they were comfortable with each other and had likely been through the process several times before.

When it was time to get down to business, I opened my thin leather attaché case and handed my resume to everyone at the table. I made sure my transcript from Harvard Extension University was in full view for anyone who wanted to see it. I later realized how ridiculous it must have looked in that setting. Angry Mr. Clean took a quick scan of my resume and asked the first question with a pained expression.

"Why do you want to do this?"

"I've wanted to teach for a long time, and this is a great opportunity," I answered enthusiastically.

"Would it bother you to work in a prison setting?" Sarah asked politely.

"Not at all," I answered, trying to look as if I had a great deal of familiarity as to what went on in a prison.

Mr. Clean and Sarah shuffled through papers for a few minutes while Richard sat there, sizing me up and grinning. He never asked a single question. The interview lasted all of eight minutes, at which time they asked if I had any questions. I had three.

"Have you had any success stories?" My first question was met with vacant looks.

"We don't keep up with people once they leave here," Frank said.

That surprised me. My schooling had taught me that a system with no feedback was a bad system. *What's the point of doing this if we don't know if it's working?* Apparently, I had a lot to learn.

"Are there any measurable objectives I should get my students to attain?"

Sarah explained the class was pass/fail, and attendance counted for 70 percent of the grade.

Basically, if you show up, you pass, I thought. *And where else do they have to go? They're in prison.*

"What materials do you have for me to use?"

After a brief silence, Richard remembered the former instructor had used some *Financial Peace* books by Dave Ramsey that still sat in a cabinet.

"We trust you to use your best judgment as far as the material goes," Sarah explained.

I started doing the math in my head. The entrepreneurship class would meet for nine hours a week for eleven weeks. That was ninety-nine hours of material I'd have to create from scratch.

"Did the former instructor leave a syllabus or any exams they used?"

I received another round of blank looks.

I realized I was pretty far down the rabbit hole at that point and stopped asking questions. Since they seemed to have run out of questions for me, I thanked them for their consideration and reiterated how much I'd love to teach the entrepreneurship class. The interview was nothing like I had prepared for, but I was silently relieved that no one seemed to have discovered the big hole in my resume: I had no teaching experience whatsoever.

We took a walking tour of the prison next. Some of the buildings went back to the 1930s, including a series of old white brick bunkhouses with thick metal doors and tinted roll-out windows, obstructing the view of what was going on inside. I learned later that only one of the four bunkhouses had air conditioning, which had to make for difficult sleeping in the summer.

Walking through the prison camp for the first time was a unique experience. My first impression was that someone spent a lot of time and money on landscaping. Up close, the prison yard was even better landscaped than I'd first noticed from the outside. Scattered throughout the entire encampment were patches of daisies, tulips, and pansies all mixed together with a budding sunflower centered perfectly in the mix. Patches of white and red perennial flowers were perfectly groomed and laid out in a well-planned order. Every building had a perimeter of manicured forest grass tufts on a bed of thick black mulch. There wasn't a weed in sight. I'd been to botanical gardens that weren't as well-designed or tended.

My second impression was of the inmates themselves. Most looked like all they did during the day was lift weights and drink protein shakes. The racial mix seemed to run about 80 percent Black and 20 percent white, and there was no shortage of tattoos, dreadlocks, or stern expressions. Everyone wearing the matching army-green pants and gray T-shirts, made them look like a platoon of well-conditioned soldiers who'd recently gone AWOL. A few guys wore a prison-issued green hunting cap with ear flaps, which from the back made them look like an oversized Elmer Fudd.

The inmates seemed to be able to move around freely in the yard. Men walked in and out of the bunkhouses and stood in small groups against the walls of the buildings. The wooden carport with the rusty free weights was a popular spot. The three weight benches were all in use with a line of guys waiting their turn. The basketball court had picked up a few more players and was alive with provocative chatter. Men sat at the plastic benches and talked or read. The speckled hound I'd noticed at the front gate was awake and sitting in the shade where ten or so men stood in line at a window, apparently waiting to buy whatever was for sale.

The prison yard had narrow sidewalks between the buildings, and the rest of the yard consisted of patches of fine gravel. An occasional guard would appear from one of the buildings, then disappear around a corner. They looked completely at ease with their surroundings, and I noticed one who stopped and shared a word with an inmate, like old friends would do. From what I could tell, the guards were unarmed. If being in a yard full of felons bothered them, I couldn't tell. They looked completely comfortable with their surroundings—as if they were strolling around their own backyards on a cool Sunday morning.

I had a lot of preconceived notions about prison from what I'd read and seen on TV. I realized the place was minimum security, but I didn't think there was any way three middle-aged guys were going to escort a pretty blond like Sarah around without, at the least, the inmates giving her long stares. As we approached a group, they lowered their heads and stepped off the sidewalk and onto the gravel to let us pass. Incredibly, I didn't see anyone make even a sideways glance at Sarah. She seemed to be oblivious to her surroundings as she calmly walked through the prison yard and chatted with Richard.

Our first stop was the sergeant's office, a small room inside one of the older bunkhouses with a service counter and a wall of small black-and-white security TVs showing the inside of the prison. A uniformed guard sat at a desk behind the counter facing the tiny TV screens, and another sat at a desk directly behind the counter with an ancient-looking desktop microphone. The two desks crammed inside the small room left almost no remaining floor space.

"You need to know where this is," Mr. Clean spoke. "There's a bathroom here you can use. You're not allowed in any part of the bunk rooms, including their bathrooms."

Richard exchanged comfortable pleasantries with one of the guards, an interaction that seemed second nature. Meanwhile, an elderly Black man in prison garb silently mopped the tiny bathroom adjoining the office, his head lowered. I figured he was disinterested and likely somewhere else altogether.

Next, we visited B Dorm, the oldest building in the prison. It was a small, white, high-ceilinged brick building built in the 1930s—appropriately with prison labor. Mr. Clean was quick to show me two big hooks embedded in the ceiling and explained that back in the day, guards would chain misbehaving prisoners and whip them. There were at least eight Black inmates in the bunk room listening and watching, and I immediately thought Mr. Clean had committed a major faux pas with the slavery overtones of chains and whips. Although I expected some sort of overt reaction from the men in the bunkhouse, no one even blinked.

"This is an honor camp," Mr. Clean volunteered as we collectively walked to the next prison attraction on our tour. "You've got to earn your way in here, and we stay full at 254 inmates. We've actually got a waiting list of people who'd like to be here."

I nodded like I understood what he was talking about as we walked side by side along the narrow sidewalk. I had no idea prisons had waiting lists, another surprise in a day full of them.

Mr. Clean continued. "This is one of the best camps in the state to get work release, so I don't put up with any troublemakers. If there's any trouble, I transfer everyone involved so they can go be someone else's problem."

"What's work release?" I asked naively. That almost coaxed a smile out of Mr. Clean, who suddenly seemed to be enjoying himself.

"We send these guys to the local factories, usually to work the third shift. If a guy gets work, he's got to pay us for room, board, and transportation, so it's good for the prison, but it's really good for the inmate. Some guys leave here with $20,000 to $30,000 from work release," he explained. "They get to keep the money, but they can't get too much of it until they're released."

Once again, I had no idea what he was talking about. My understanding of prison labor was guys busting rocks for ten cents an hour.

"We have about sixty guys on work release right now," he said. "You'll get to meet some of them. In fact, most of them will be sleeping in the same dorm where you'll be teaching."

We passed another bunkhouse that resembled the others, then the building with the window that appeared to be a store of sorts and had a line of men out front. What looked like a menu with a price list was taped to the wall next to the window. Near that building was a tiny white brick structure that served as the medical facility across the yard from our next stop: G Dorm. Compared to the other buildings, G Dorm was a modern marvel: a raised prefabricated aluminum building with a concrete ramp for the entrance. Its aluminum door opened into a dayroom, which was about twenty feet square and had a musty, watered-down bleach smell.

The dayroom had a chipped black-and-white checkerboard tile floor. An opening on the wall immediately to the right led to a long bunk room that made up most of the structure. Two long rows of steel bunkbeds, each equipped with a small locker built into the bedframe, lined opposing walls.

"This is the classroom," Richard said, breaking his silence. "I won't be here on the days you teach, so before you start class, you'll want to roll the partition into the doorway so the guys can sleep. The ones in this dorm work the night shift, so they'll be asleep in here while you're teaching."

This is the classroom? You gotta be kidding me!

Three older men and one young man sat at various tables and stared at small wall-mounted silent TVs. Each had what looked to be a clear-cased transistor radio on the table with a white earbud cord running into one of their ears. They had barely looked up when we entered the room. Between the two TVs was a table with a microwave. A young, tattooed, light-skinned man stood in front of it, waiting for whatever he was cooking inside. The only sounds in the room were the whine of the small window air conditioner and the dull hum of the microwave. Men in prison garb walked freely between the dayroom and the bunk room. The dayroom had eleven square tables with fading checkerboards laminated on them that faced two small TVs hanging on the far wall. Two pay telephones were attached to the wall next to the bunk room entrance, with signs listing the phone's operating hours and notifying users that all calls were recorded. Conspicuous white security cameras were mounted in adjacent corners. Anything that happened in the room could be watched back in the sergeant's office. In the far corner was a crooked, wheeled marker board with a portrait orientation.

"I leave the marker board in the programs office, so you'll have to wheel it over here before class and back to the office when you're through," Richard said. "If you're like me, you'll probably use that board a lot."

The hosts studied my face, perhaps waiting for some sort of shocked reaction and a dash for the gate. While visualizing how the dingy dayroom could be converted into some sort of learning space, I realized how vulnerable I would be in my "classroom." I'd be the only noninmate in the whole building, and no member of the prison staff would be within earshot. There would be ten students in my class and nothing but a saggy partition separating me from the other forty or so convicted felons in the bunk room.

If anyone wants to get violent in here, I've got no allies, no exits, and no way to call for help.

Remembering the ninety-nine hours of content I lacked, I asked Richard if I could show videos on the two small TVs.

"If you want to show videos, you'll need to make arrangements to show them in the chapel," Richard explained.

I thought it best to not ask any more questions and act like I'd done all of it before. *You gotta start somewhere.*

But I had serious doubts about teaching four-and-a-half-hour classes twice a week with no preexisting material, no internet access, and no PowerPoint all by myself while surrounded by men serving prison sentences. The thought of thanking everyone for their time and making a beeline back to my normal life in Charlotte never crossed my mind, though. It was the closest I'd gotten to being a teacher, and there was no way I was going to turn it down.

Because I hadn't openly shown any concerns and was doing my best to look cool and competent, we walked back to the programs office to adjourn our meeting. Richard wanted to show me where my lone teaching aid, the Dave Ramsey books, were kept. He disappeared behind a wall for a few seconds and returned with the schedule for the next class attached to a brown clipboard.

"Are there any Thursdays or Fridays you can't work through July?" he asked.

I thought Richard was jumping the gun since they hadn't had a chance to discuss hiring me outside of my presence, but no one made any sort of objection. I was too good of a salesman to not try to close the deal.

"My wife and I have a trip to Ireland planned in the middle of June," I said. "But other than that, I can be here every day you need me to be."

And just like that, Richard wrote my name into the schedule with a felt-tipped pen.

This interview couldn't have gone any better.

My career in sales had taught me to always be on the lookout for closing signals from a prospective customer—telltales that a customer was ready to agree to your deal. By writing my name on the schedule, Richard gave me the biggest closing signal of all time.

I'd also learned that once a deal was struck, it was time for the salesperson to end the meeting and get out of the door as quickly and gracefully as possible. Nothing good happened by hanging around once you got everything you set out to get. In fact, two really bad things could happen if you stayed: The prospect could talk himself out of the deal or, worse yet, the salesperson could talk the prospect out of the deal. My instincts told me it was time to go because there was no way I could improve the situation. I'd gotten everything I came for and was looking for the fastest way out of the programs office.

Sarah asked if I had any further questions before she left, and despite my urge to leave, my self-preservation instincts were slightly tougher, so I hesitantly asked about riot protocol. Mr. Clean shot me an amused look and told me I didn't have to worry about any rioting. I'd just walked through an army of strong and mostly angry-looking young men, and I'd heard of prison riots before, so it seemed like there should be a procedure in place. I wasn't panicking about potential problems I might face, but I wanted to know what I should do.

I inserted again in my calmest voice, "If I'm going to be in that room by myself the whole time, I'd like to know what I should do if things get out of hand."

Richard again did his best to assure me that nothing like

that would happen, so I let it pass for the time being. Sarah headed back to the college and Mr. Clean went into his office, leaving Richard to escort me.

Since I had time alone with Richard, I asked again about the riot protocol.

Richard just grinned and restated, “You don’t have to worry about anything like that.”

“I’m going to take the job either way, Richard,” I told him. “But I’d feel a lot better if I knew what I should do when we have a problem.”

“I’ve been here over twenty years,” Richard explained. “We’ve never had anything like that happen. Maybe some pushing and shoving a time or two, but that’s about it.”

He led me out of the programs office past another amazing floral arrangement and to the gate leading to the side parking lot. He opened the gate, shook my hand, and locked the gate behind me as soon as I was on the other side. I stood facing him, and he could obviously read the confusion and disbelief on my face.

Richard gave me a bemused look though the chain link and said, “I know this was a lot for you to take in, but believe it or not, you’ll get used to it.”

CHAPTER TWO

Know from Whence You Came

"Know from whence you came. If you know whence you came, there are absolutely no limitations to where you can go."

—James Baldwin, American novelist

MY FATHER WAS BORN AND raised in the gritty blue-collar town of Aurora, Illinois, where he met my mom and was the starting center for the high school basketball team. His teammates nicknamed him "Ladder" because he was six foot six and so skinny you could count his ribs. My dad received a basketball scholarship to a nearby college, but after a short stay, decided it wasn't for him. He returned home and got a job in a local metal fabrication factory that made an assortment of metal storage products, including shelving, racks, and lockers. It was a union factory, and they hired my father for the entry-level job of welding metal legs to workbenches. That was piece work, so in addition to an hourly wage, they paid my father a fixed sum for every bench he completed.

My dad was young, ambitious, and had a pregnant wife at home, so his goal was to make as much money as he could every shift. After a few days, the shop foreman cautioned him to slow down.

"If you keep going at your current pace, they're going to raise our daily quotas," the foreman warned.

My father didn't slow down, and the foreman's warnings proved prescient. My dad was fired. On his way to the pay window for his last check, he encountered one of his own father's friends in the office, someone who recognized him from his basketball glory days.

"Ladder, what did you do to get fired?" the man asked.

"I was going too fast and making too much money," my dad explained.

The family friend then said the words that made all the difference in my father's life and the following generations. "Maybe you don't belong out in the shop then, Ladder. Maybe we should put you in sales. You can make all the money you want to in sales."

The vice president of sales started my father in the worst sales territory available: West Virginia. Through hard work and determination, he worked his way to more productive territories in Pennsylvania and Georgia and was eventually chosen to open a new territory for the company in Charlotte, North Carolina, in the early '70s. With his refined sales tactics and natural ability to persuade, he developed the uncharted region into one of the top-producing territories in the country year after year. Charlotte also became the first place that felt like home to a family that then included me at age five, my parents, and my two older sisters. We moved from a small apartment in Atlanta to a big five-bedroom house on a half-acre lot in Charlotte. The big backyard and friendly neighbors made us feel like we were finally in a place where we could plant roots, especially after my brother was born shortly after.

My father's job required extensive travel. He was typically gone for two weeks and then home for the next two. His inconsistent presence left the disciplinary action of four small children to my mother, who had no interest or abilities in that department. Instead of handling our misdeeds as they happened, she waited for my father's return, informed him of our transgressions for the past two weeks, and stepped back while we stood with our heads bowed waiting to receive our belated punishment—always a firm spanking. That peculiar style of parenting taught me to lead a sort of dual life; because my punishment was always deferred, I could do as I pleased while my dad was gone. Once I'd crossed the line, there was no point in trying to behave anymore since I was only going to be spanked once, no matter how severe my wrongdoing. When my father was home, I tried to be on my best behavior and have as little interaction with the stern disciplinarian as possible. With his size and unpredictable temperament, he was an intimidating figure. His fits of anger seemed to be completely random and would send us kids scrambling for a safe haven. It led me to spend a lot of time outdoors in the shadowy woods near our home. I became active in the Boy Scouts and looked forward to the overnight camping trips away from the fray.

As a powerless child, I did what I could to try to control my environment. My father's unpredictable disposition provided me with an early opportunity to read body language and voice inflections, and I excelled at it in the hope of keeping a lid on his simmering anger. It was a losing battle, of course. Nothing I did made any difference, but it gave me a lot of practice, and the people-reading skills I gained became valuable tools in my future endeavors—personally and in business. The authoritarian style of parenting I experienced was commonplace at that time. Children were expected to be seen and not heard, and no one was shielded from life's challenges. Difficulties were there to build character.

My father would be the first to admit that if he'd stayed in Charlotte, he probably would've retired as a sales manager for the same company in which he started as a shop welder. In the late '80s, however, he was presented with an opportunity he couldn't pass up: the position of national sales manager. The promotion required a return to the company's home office in Illinois, and my father headed back north, family in tow.

My siblings and I were completely blindsided by the move to the Midwest after laying down roots for seven years in Charlotte. I had little time to pack my belongings, much less say goodbye to my longtime friends. With little preparation, I was forced to start eighth grade in the small midwestern city, where the blue-collar kids would often make fun of my Southern accent. To them, North Carolinians were all redneck hicks who lived in trailer parks.

Winter's mounting snowbanks and bitter cold eliminated any possibility of the outdoor activities that had provided a reprieve in Charlotte and played such a big role in my upbringing. Tension grew at home; my father wasn't traveling anymore, and he came home in worse and worse moods. The frozen Illinois cornfields offered me no place to hide.

The only upside to the move was the time I got to spend with my grandparents. My grandmother lived through the Great Depression, which taught her to be frugal. She used to ask for aluminum foil for her Christmas present and never tired of spending time with her grandchildren, doing whatever they wanted to do. The interest my grandparents showed in their four grandchildren provided us with the feeling of worth we so desperately needed. Instead of their annual visit at Christmas, we saw them weekly. My siblings and I cherished the newfound time with them.

At the insistence of my mother, I joined a Boy Scout troop, but it was much different from my mannerly troop back in North Carolina. Instead of polite Southern kids who were taught to respect nature and always leave a campsite cleaner than you found it, the new group consisted of uncontrollable brats who used a picnic table for firewood on the first campout

I attended. I got within six months of earning the Eagle Scout award and begged my mom to let me quit. My mother hated quitters and insisted I see it through. I came home the night it was finally over and unceremoniously put the small eagle-embossed cloth badge on her nightstand. I'd earned it for her, not me. But her refusing to let me quit set a precedent that carried over to other parts of my life and became a great gift. I soon realized achieving the rank of Eagle Scout was a rarity—it impressed a lot of people. If I'd not been grounded in the importance of sticking it out when things were hard, I never would've made it as far as I did professionally or personally.

Aurora only had two high schools, and I was soon walking the same halls of the building where my father had demonstrated his prowess on the basketball court. He'd pushed me to be an athlete since I was old enough to bounce a ball, but I always failed miserably. His authoritarian style of coaching made me apprehensive and fearful. Childhood memories of him pacing the sideline and criticizing my efforts remained fresh. I tried out for the basketball team my sophomore year to appease him and silently celebrated as I stood in front of the cut sheet, realizing I hadn't made the team. I joined the swim team instead. My dad didn't know anything about swimming, and I figured even if he wanted to come to the meet and yell instructions at me, my head would be underwater most of the time.

The best thing to come out of my time in Aurora was a neighbor named Kurt, who lived a few doors down. I met him while walking to school one day when his mom stopped her car and offered me a ride. Like me, Kurt was a recent transfer to town. We didn't fit in with the cliquish kids who'd been going to school together since kindergarten and were convinced Aurora was the center of the universe. Kurt was raised by a Marine Corps drill instructor, which gave him both an edgy toughness and a disdain for authority. His mostly unsupervised home provided an escape from my turbulent home life. Together, we discovered country music, alcohol, and girls and spent our summers working a variety of minimum wage jobs. Kurt was nine months older than me, and as soon as he got his driver's license, he drove us to Chicago every chance we got, the two of us piling in his parents' beige Delta Eighty-Eight. We explored parts of the Windy City that weren't on anyone's tourist map and somehow seemed to know just how far we could bend the rules before there were consequences.

Kurt and I went our separate ways for college but joined forces that first summer to seek employment. Due to our complete lack of marketable skills, the best job we could find our first time back was a long three-month sentence as plumber's apprentices. We spent that summer bent over ditches, smearing tar, and wrapping copper water pipes with pipe tape in the hot Illinois sun for a paltry $3.35 an hour. We left work every day sweaty, tired, and covered with sticky black goo. Standing shoulder-deep in a foul-smelling ditch on our last day, we vowed to find better jobs when we returned home from college the following year.

The next school year passed quickly, and although I wasn't old enough to legally drink alcohol—much less serve it—I convinced the manager of a local tavern to hire me as a cocktail waiter the following summer. The bar was part of a Mexican restaurant and featured live music on the weekends. I thought working in air conditioning, earning tips, and listening to bands would be a lot more enjoyable than the plumbing experience, and the late hours would keep the daylight hours free. Although the bar had previously used only waitresses, I persuaded the manager to give me a chance. Shortly after he hired me, I convinced him to hire Kurt, too. That summer, we spent our days at Wrigley Field or canoeing on the nearby Fox River and our nights working in the smoky bar, listening to bands, earning tips, and meeting girls. The summer of 1984 was the best of my life.

While I was busy living it up that summer, my father's "safe" job at the locker company was coming to a quick and unceremonious finish. What my dad didn't know when he accepted the promotion that brought us to Aurora was that there were malicious plans afoot at the home office. Because it was a publicly traded company, the newly appointed president had plans to financially damage the company in order to lower the stock share price so that he could buy enough to become the majority shareholder. My dad had unknowingly put himself right in the line of fire between the old guard and a few immoral corporate raiders.

He first realized the end of his career was approaching on the day he was looking at the inventory list on a database, trying to fill an order for a common shelving part. The computer showed none in the warehouse. My father knew that couldn't be true, so he went to physically check and found hundreds of the parts stacked almost to the ceiling. He dutifully reported the discrepancy to the new president. When he returned to work the next day, a chain-link fence blocked the office entrance to the warehouse with a fresh sign stating the new company policy: office personnel were no longer allowed in the warehouse.

It was just a matter of time before the people in charge forced him to leave the company he'd spent more than twenty-five years building. The president put him in charge of selling their unproductive laundry locker line to hasten his exit. As my father's final act, he sold the product to uniform companies far and wide, filling the system with so many orders that the company fell six months behind in production. With nothing left to sell, he handed in his resignation.

At that time, my father was in his early fifties and had always worked for someone else. After powerlessly watching an outsider dismantle the business he'd invested decades in, he decided he'd only work for himself from that point forward.

My dad paid for my first two years of college, but knowing his secure job was gone, I offered to pay for the rest of my education. I didn't see a big future in Aurora and was looking for a fresh start somewhere else. My oldest sister had moved back to Charlotte and gotten married as soon as her last year of high school was over, and she agreed to let me live in her basement for a small rent payment until I could get on my feet.

My father took a job as an independent sales agent for a company that competed with his old one and started his own small business in Charlotte. The decision made a lot of sense. He'd be working in the same territory where he'd had so much success a decade before with the same product he'd been selling for most of his life. He'd built a lot of important relationships with people in the industry. The thought of converting some of his former employer's big customers over to the competition had to be a great motivator.

He started his business, McLaughlin and Associates, with almost no resources. He went from living in an upscale five-bedroom suburban home and driving a Cadillac to living in a run-down furnished apartment on the bad side of town and driving an old van. I never heard him complain about his change in lifestyle, though. Being his own boss more than compensated for the material things he gave up for his freedom.

I'd been waiting tables for a year when my father returned to town. My time away at college and a year of living in different cities had put more than physical distance between us. As I was taking care of myself for the first time, I was realizing there was more to my dad than just his role as the overbearing authority figure of my childhood. He started at the bottom of a company and worked his way up the ladder, sacrificing part of himself to provide for his family.

I planned to rent an apartment near the college campus when classes started that fall. When dad arrived, we were both looking for a good roommate. We decided to get an apartment together in a sketchy neighborhood not too far from the university. I insisted on paying half the rent, which I felt would buy my freedom to come and go as I pleased. We each got a bedroom, and the small dining room served as the headquarters for his start-up company.

My dad traveled his old sales territory and worked incessantly. I went to school during the days and worked nights at a local bar. Our dining room furniture consisted of a desk, a phone, and an old filing cabinet. It was from there he did his sales prospecting, which was my first opportunity to see him at work. I learned that my father was a master persuader. After hours of hearing him work deals from the next room, I was genuinely impressed with his ability to get his prospect to do what he wanted. He seemed to know exactly when to apply pressure and when to lay back and let the customer do the talking, much like a fisherman who knows when it's time to set the hook or let the fish take some line. He could read the intentions of the person and steer them where he wanted in such an affable manner that they didn't mind going there. What my father did for a living had always been a mystery to me. I was seeing him with new eyes, a master mired in the tiny dining room of a ramshackle apartment, his artistry on this new canvas shining bright all the same.

My foray into sales began with one year of college remaining. One of my dad's former colleagues, Myron, had a business selling glare screens for computers and was looking for distributors. My father thought it would be a great opportunity for me to learn how to sell and that we might make a few dollars along the way. Myron had found a supplier of computer glare screens, which were basically dark nylon mesh cut to certain popular computer monitor sizes and glued to a plastic frame. It was back in the days of DOS and cathode-ray tubes with bright green lettering, which made reading for long periods of time difficult, especially in an environment with bright overhead lighting or nearby windows.

Myron's technique consisted of physically cold calling the local business parks. The goal was to leave a screen for the prospect to try at no charge and return in two weeks to either collect the screen or make the sale. The screens sold for $39.95 each, and each sale yielded about a 50 percent commission.

Myron took me out one afternoon to make cold calls, and I had the pleasure of watching a master salesman in action. Much like my father on the phone, Myron had a knack for making people like him right away. He instinctively knew when to push a little harder and when to walk away. We made seven or eight cold calls that day, and Myron left behind screens with four potential customers. After we left a prospect, Myron would provide insights in his soft Georgia accent.

"That should be a good one," he said. "You should get an order when you follow that one up." Or "That's a regional office, which makes this one a tough sale. They'd have to get approval."

Myron sold my dad and me a starter kit of samples to hand out and a last shot of confidence to me. "You're a lot younger and a lot better-looking than me," he said. "You're going to do great."

Since my last college class of the week met on Friday mornings, I began spending every Friday afternoon visiting business parks and learning the art of cold-call selling by trial and error. The elation I felt at turning a cold prospect into a repeat customer was unlike anything I'd ever experienced. That feeling couldn't happen unless I opened the first door, and no one else could take credit for the customer base I was building. I had to earn them one at time.

One Friday afternoon, I happened to walk into the local office of Dun & Bradstreet, a nationwide company that offered business-to-business credit reports. Instead of receiving the typical brush-off after listening to my pitch, the receptionist welcomed me in and explained they were in the process of evaluating some computer glare screens. She ushered me through a big room full of employees sitting at desks and staring into computer monitors to the branch manager's office, who had one of Myron's brochures on his desk along with a price quote.

"We're considering buying a substantial amount of these. What can you do about the price?" the man asked.

I was very new to selling and didn't know what to do. I had programmed myself to leave the screen and make a quick exit, so this was unfamiliar territory. I said something about needing to check with my boss, took his business card, and got out of there as quickly as I could, trying desperately not to show my complete confusion.

I returned home and explained what happened to my father, who instantly lit up, took the man's card, and grabbed for the phone.

"He just wants a better deal," he explained while hurriedly dialing the phone number. Within minutes, my father closed the deal, which earned me over a thousand dollars in commission. I'd never held a check with my name and so many zeros on it, and that experience went a long way toward igniting a fire for a career in sales. It also taught me I could learn a lot more about business from my father than I was in my business classes at the local university.

When I was a kid and asked what I was going to be when I grew up, I'd say I was going to work for my dad as a salesman. My parents thought that was an impossibility. He'd worked for one company for most of his life, and they couldn't see any scenario where I'd work for him. No one ever tried to talk me out of my plans, though, and years later, the opportunity actually presented itself. My father had apparently decided we worked well together, and the thought of doubling his small company's sales efforts must've appealed to him. As I started my senior year in college, he asked if I'd be interested in working for him after graduation.

"We're just starting out, and my company doesn't really have any money," he explained. "But I can afford to buy you a company car, and I think we'll have a lot of fun working together."

Despite our differences during my younger years, I realized it was a golden opportunity. My father was a master at his craft and had a loyal customer base in place.

"I'll do it," I told him. "But just to be clear, I'll give it two years, then I'll have to find something safer."

At the time, I thought I was taking a huge risk. I might spend the next two years investing my time and energy into a start-up that could easily go south and have nothing to show for it. What I realized later was the same thing my dad had learned the hard way: the real risk in business was putting your future in someone else's hands.

Earning commissions was much more rewarding than the seemingly pointless letter grades they handed out in college. With one semester to go, I approached my dad and explained I'd completed all the business courses I needed for my degree. I had eighteen hours of electives left and could see no point in grinding out another four months of meaningless classes and working at the bar downtown for minimum wage when I could instead be making some real money.

"I'm ready to get started now," I told him.

My father didn't agree with my plan. "You're too close to quit now. You've invested too much time and money to not come out of there with a degree. Four months is nothing in the big picture, and you might need that degree someday." Much like my mother did when I was ready to quit the Boy Scouts, my father convinced me to finish what I started. And just like my mom, he was right.

Our relationship had come a long way by that point due to us working and living together in an isolated apartment with almost no resources. We'd developed a sort of "us against the world" mentality. As much as I didn't want to finish college, I did what he suggested. It was one of the best pieces of fatherly wisdom I received at the time, though there was much more of that to come.

I had my final class on a Friday morning in April 1987. I'd moved in with Kurt, who had come to Charlotte to visit for a week and decided to stay. We had a graduation party planned for that night, so I asked my dad if it was okay to start working for him first thing Monday morning. Although it seemed like a simple request, my first instruction was to report for work directly after my last class ended. I drove across town to his small apartment to find him loading his golf clubs in his van.

"I need you to be in the office," he explained. "I've got a game scheduled with some customers this afternoon."

I plopped into the seat at the lone desk and irritably asked what he wanted me to do. He hurriedly looked around the small dining room until he found his address book.

"Why don't you copy this?" he instructed. "You'll need these contacts."

I sat alone in his dining room on a beautiful spring afternoon, copying names and numbers, listening to a wall clock tick off the hours of my first day on the job while my friends were celebrating their impending graduation at a pool party. The only upside to the misspent afternoon was that the phone never rang. I had no idea what I would've said if a customer called.

CHAPTER THREE
Surviving the Storm

> *"Sometimes, we're tested not to show our weaknesses, but to discover our strengths."*
>
> —Unknown

I LOOK BACK ON THE time working with my father as a tremendous gift. Despite the rocky relationship we had in my childhood, he didn't hold anything back in teaching me the ways of the industrial storage product business. We spent workdays in our makeshift office, which was newly equipped with an electric Old Style beer light on the wall. One of my first lessons was not to focus on the size of the potential order but instead on its profit. Together, we set a monthly goal of making a $10,000 profit. On the occasional months we reached our goal, we'd ignite the beer light and bask in its fluorescent glow. There were many occasions we were close to our profit goal at the end of the month, and my dad would be talking to a customer on the phone. He'd wave to get my attention and start pointing at the beer light to let me know he was about to make the sale that would put us over the top. "We're going to make it!" his thumbs-up and raised eyebrows would silently convey. Meanwhile, his voice never altered.

Although it was a meager existence, the early years when my father and I worked together were priceless. We shared the struggles and the triumphs that played a huge role in a start-up business. We worked together for five years, and I learned more in those five years than at any other time in my life. My father had been a sales manager most of his career, and he was a tough grader. He taught me that in a sales situation, you either got an *A* or an *F*. There were no middle grades. If you came away with the order, you got an *A*. Any other result was a failure.

My father placed all the emphasis on making sales and keeping costs low for his company. Record keeping was a low priority. I initially tried to set up a manual accounting system, but some of his liberal business expenses were impossible to categorize, and I soon gave up. My business education taught me enough to know that playing fast and loose with the numbers could only lead to trouble, and I tried on occasion to warn him that we were defenseless if we were ever audited.

"Don't worry," he explained. "I've got a shoebox full of receipts, and if we're ever audited, I'll take them in and pour them all over the guy's desk."

Armed with that wily contingency plan, we bravely moved forward. Naturally, we *were* soon audited. It started out innocently enough as a sales tax audit from the state of North Carolina, but when we couldn't get our bank receipts to match the sales numbers we reported on our tax return, things began to heat up. I decided to handle the audit, thinking it was better if we gave them one version of what we'd done instead of two, and I didn't want my dad in there with his box of receipts.

I dragged the audit out for as long as possible, but the day came when the head auditor called me in for a meeting and calmly informed me that they planned to contact the IRS regarding our fictitious numbers. With no other options, I had to throw myself to their mercy, explaining our predicament to a middle-aged woman with emotionless eyes. I told her my father had no formal business education and had played fast and loose with his record keeping, and although I initially tried, I sat by, powerless to make any accounting changes. I promised her that, if given another chance, we'd shut down our company and never darken their door again. My last resolve was to try to make myself cry. Fortunately, it never came to that.

For no other reason than pure sympathy, they agreed to let us off the hook in exchange for payment of the owed sales tax and our promise to go and sin no more. We shut down McLaughlin and Associates and steered customers to our new enterprise, Lockers Unlimited.

We'd learned over the past five years that instead of trying to sell the whole product line, the locker sale took the most skill, and it was where we made the majority of our profit. Part of the transition to forming the new company was the decision that I'd be the sole owner and president. My father was still active as the sales agent for our main supplier and helped with day-to-day operations, but he gradually took a less active role. I relocated my company from the dining room to the smallest available unit in a run-down business park, bought a fax machine, and brought in Kurt to help in the office and handle our installations.

Those actions all went against my dad's incessant advice of keeping the company overhead low, but I thought there was space to grow. He'd given me great guidance over the years, but I was in charge now, and I saw the potential for bigger things. I could never measure up to my father's expectations on the basketball court, but in the sales arena, I'd learned I could.

Our sales rose significantly in less than a year, and I moved the company to a much larger unit in the same business park. Kurt was a big reason for it. He could handle any problem in the field, and the locker business was teeming with problems. Like all middlemen, we were completely reliant on someone else making the product we sold correctly and on time. Once our product shipped, we were at the mercy of long-haul carriers, who'd often damage or lose our product. When it arrived, we had to cooperate with the powers that be at construction sites to make the installation go smoothly. I used to say it was easy for me to tell a prospective customer how good the buying experience was going to be, but it was Kurt who made it happen. His raw toughness gave me strength when I needed it, and he was always there when I needed him. I made him a 20 percent owner in the business against his objections, and he never let me down.

Two years into the existence of my company, my father came into the office and sat thoughtfully in silence for a few minutes. Then, he said he was proud of me. His words jolted me like a shot of electricity. It was as if the enormous weight of not living up to his expectations on the basketball court in my youth had instantly been lifted from my shoulders. The turbulent childhood experiences taught me to take on responsibility and made me goal-oriented. With my father's encouragement and guidance, I felt like I could accomplish anything.

* * *

My drive to build a successful company left little time for socializing, and I'd been cautious with women up to that point. I had little income and what I considered to be a shaky future. I was never looking for a serious relationship, but I found one by doing something completely out of character: I joined a dating service, paying for six introductions. A few days later, a yellow card with the name "Rebecca Freeman" came in the mail. I thought I could foresee what lay ahead for me. There was something about the card that felt special.

I called the number and talked for hours to the warmest, funniest, and most down-to-earth person I'd ever spoken to.

We agreed on our first date: a night of bowling and a meal at a local diner. I walked up the concrete steps to her apartment door on the big night and found myself swept away by her gentle nature and sweet smile. Reba was the first girl to pass my "What do you want to do with your life?" test. Whenever a woman would ask me, I took it as a sign she was trying to get a glimpse of her life if she stayed with me. My answer was "Sell used cars." It painted such an undesirable potential future that my prospects had all stopped answering my calls. Not Reba, though.

"I think you'd be great at that," she said, her blue-green eyes staring at me, unwavering.

I spent that Thanksgiving with Reba's family and learned why we were such kindred souls. Thanksgiving was held at her grandma's tiny house in a "mill village," where the local textile mill employed the majority of the population. Grandma's claim to fame was that she'd once chased a black bear out of her garden with her kitchen broom. I couldn't wait to meet her.

As we approached the front of her small, one-story house, Grandma floated to the door and warmly welcomed me into her tiny living room full of doilies and knickknacks. She spent the next hour or so regaling me with stories of her childhood in the North Carolina mountains. Dressed in a patterned housecoat partially covered by a worn apron, she had a gift for smiling with her voice and would occasionally interrupt her story to spit snuff into an empty peach can. She shared the same sweet but firm disposition as my grandmother, and I felt completely comfortable in her presence.

Reba had experienced a turbulent upbringing at home as well, and her grandmother also had stepped in to provide support and direction. After that day, I wanted nothing more than to spend the rest of my life with Reba, someone I felt like I completely understood. Our grandmothers only met once, at our wedding, but they stood proudly together after the ceremony, sharing a look of accomplishment—two strong women who both stepped up for their families when needed.

Over the next three years, my company experienced solid growth, and I decided to move into a 10,000 square-foot building in an upscale business park on the west side of Charlotte. I was eager to leave the run-down industrial park on the bad side of town, and I felt sure the company was ready. It was a huge leap, but we needed the space. I was confident the profits could easily cover the $3,250 monthly rent, so much so that I signed a five-year unbreakable lease.

Shortly after the ink dried on my lease, though, things went south. We experienced the Y2K scare, causing our primary manufacturer to hurriedly adopt a new order entry system when they became convinced none of their metal-stamping machines were going to work on January 1, 2000. They never got the new system to work correctly, and our in-house orders were significantly compromised. Locker jobs began shipping months late with incorrect or missing parts. My loyal customer base became irate, and my company's sales began decreasing for the first time.

We had just recovered from that unforeseen debacle when 9/11 happened. Our business came to a screeching halt while we all waited to see the next target for terrorism. I watched helplessly as our bottom line consistently shrank month to month and then year to year.

As if that wasn't enough, the new factory representative decided to set up one of our installers to compete with us. The new entrant was cutting a step out of my distribution channel, quoting prices to contractors that were way below the standard in order to gain market share with the intent of putting us out of business. Things got so bad that I became convinced we couldn't recover. I worked in the building by myself, hoping to squeeze out enough profit to make the next rent payment. With two years left on the lease, I didn't see much of a future, so I enlisted a business broker to place a value on my company and started to look for a buyer.

I thought it fair to explain my decision to Kurt since he was a part owner. His reaction surprised me.

"If you want to sell the company, you can have my shares of stock for free," he said. "But what are we going to do then?"

That was nowhere close to the reaction I anticipated. Didn't he realize how doomed we were?

Instead, he challenged me. "Look, I'll cover the office for you if you want to go out and get some new customers, but I'm not quitting."

Kurt certainly saw the situation differently, and I'd always respected his judgment.

"Fine," I said. "If you want to go down in flames, we'll go down together. Maybe that's fitting." I figured it wouldn't be long before we wouldn't have anything left to sell, but if Kurt wanted to keep fighting, there was no way I was going to abandon him.

The day I decided to stay and fight was the same day it started turning around for us. While Kurt covered the office, I cold called markets outside my competitors' reach and came away with some solid accounts. I negotiated a better discount with a competitive line and steered the majority of our business to them. The capper was when my competitor finally realized he wasn't getting enough profit in the small jobs and shifted his focus to larger projects, like new high schools, that we had no interest in pursuing. That left the small projects to us, and those were what we did best. In a short period of time, our sales and profitability reached heights we'd never seen before. The experience provided two big life lessons: the people who succeed are the people who refuse to quit, even in the bleakest of times—perhaps especially in those times. And having the right partner in business is as important as having the right partner at home.

With business booming, I once again thought I had it all figured out until the day I had a potential customer contact me about buying shelving and shipping it to India to barter for some farm equipment he needed. We agreed on a price and were ready to move forward. My new customer was much older than I was and had run many successful businesses. He asked me to send a quote to his contact in India so that he could sign off on the deal.

"What's his fax number?" I asked.

"He doesn't have a fax," he replied. "You're going to have to email it to him."

I feigned understanding and spent hours trying to figure out how to send an attachment on an email. Soon after I sent the email, I heard back from my customer, who asked what format I'd used for the quote.

"Microsoft Works," I answered. It was the same program I'd used since the days of working in the dining room of a tiny apartment nearly fifteen years prior.

"Works?" he asked. "Where did you find that old program? You've got to send it in Excel. Nobody uses Works anymore."

I had no idea what Excel was. I'd been running the business the same way for eleven years. Working for myself and mostly by myself, I found it was easy to lose track of the ever-changing and improving business tools. I was still using old software and a fax machine, which, unbeknownst to me, were becoming more and more outdated. I had to bring myself up to speed if I were to survive in the ever-evolving environment.

The factory representative who'd almost put us out of business a few years earlier complained to me that he could never go any further up the company ladder because he didn't have the MBA the company required to be considered for any upper management position.

One day, tired of his grumbling, I blurted out, “Why don’t you quit complaining and go get an MBA?”

The question I directed at him instantly seemed like a solution to my own problem. I’d never considered going back to school, but perhaps it was exactly what I needed to catch up on all the new technology I’d let pass me by. My full-time job and youthful disdain for formal education had earned me a mid-C average at UNCC sixteen years earlier, but I promptly filled out an application for their MBA program. It was a direction I’d never planned to go, but it opened the doors to a new world of opportunity and sent my life in a completely unexpected direction.

CHAPTER FOUR

Back to School

"I've learned that I still have a lot to learn."

—Maya Angelou, American poet

I WASN'T SURE HOW DIFFICULT it was to get into an MBA program, but my hope was the school would overlook those low undergraduate grades for the real-world business experience I'd gained.

An associate professor who was reviewing my application called a few weeks later. We had a lengthy conversation, and I felt good about my chances of being accepted. A week or so later, a thick envelope arrived with a letter of acceptance and a notice that mandatory orientation would be held the following Saturday morning for all members of the graduating class of 2005.

I arrived on campus that Saturday, walked in the door of the same building I had sixteen years earlier, and sat in the same seat. I'd recently turned forty and, as expected, I was by far the oldest student there. UNCC didn't have an executive MBA program, so many of my fellow students were straight out of their undergraduate program and roughly half my age. We spent the morning introducing ourselves and listening to a guest speaker explain how his business handled the 9/11 crisis. There was a networking lunch on the agenda, but I slipped out the side door instead and drove across town to help Kurt finish a locker installation at a private high school. I planned to take one class per semester at night, so I knew my MBA experience would last at least five years. There was plenty of time for networking down the road.

Returning to college was great for me, although it got off to a somewhat rough start. I was the only student to use an overhead projector for my first presentation, while everyone else had slick PowerPoint slides. I was also the only student to do research at the library for our first group project. I remember one of my group mates staring at me like I'd just hopped off a spaceship.

"You mean, you actually went inside the library?" he asked, bewildered.

I clearly was different from my fellow students, but they were always respectful. I was determined to finish the program by any means necessary. If my prematurely graying hair made me conspicuous among what eventually became the class of 2009, the fact I'd only worked for myself for the past twenty-plus years made me a true oddity. Most students were pursuing their graduate degree in order to climb the corporate ladder; meanwhile, I was there in an attempt to keep myself current in the ever-changing business environment. There was no raise or promotion waiting for me upon completion of the degree. My resume was irrelevant.

Because there were so few entrepreneurs enrolled in the MBA program, opportunities arose to guest-speak for undergraduate entrepreneurship classes. Those experiences were life-changing and awoke my inner desire to teach. I held a question-and-answer session with the would-be entrepreneurs after my first presentation and was surprised at how easily I could answer their questions and warn against some of the flawed strategies they contemplated. The principles of entrepreneurship were hard to learn from a textbook, so the best source of information was from someone who'd already traveled the road those would-be entrepreneurs were considering. All start-up enterprises began with a limited number of mistakes that could be made before costs exceeded the revenue and the music stopped. Once the money ran out, it was game over—no exceptions. My failed start-up experience, combined with my trials and tribulations in the locker business, had served as a great platform to learn both what *to* do and what *not* to do when starting and running a small business. The opportunities to instruct helped me realize there were a lot of potential small business owners with really good ideas who needed a bit of direction. I was capable of helping them.

Hands down, the best professor in the MBA program was a marketing professor named Dr. Erevelles. He had a unique gift for presenting material in a way that made students want to pay attention. His class was part entertainment, part information, and played like a well-constructed infomercial. His approach to teaching was straightforward. "If I don't have your attention, then my message is meaningless."

Most of my fellow students shared my love for Dr. Erevelles's classes. In comparison to the dry finance and economics classes, his classes were like a Vegas show. One night, he told the class he had an obscene PowerPoint presentation to show and added that anyone who might be offended was free to leave the classroom. Since he then had our undivided attention, he started a presentation titled "My Porno Collection," which consisted of pictures of the board of directors for ten of the largest American corporations.

In his Indian dialect, he shouted out, "Isn't this disgusting? They're all old white men. No wonder they can't come up with any new ideas."

The positive influence he had on his students made me

realize that teaching—when done properly—had a lifelong impact on people.

The college experience was so much more rewarding the second time around, and the impact of the principles I'd learned and applied to my business was fresh on my mind when I graduated years later. Although I'd blown off my undergraduate ceremony, I was there in cap and gown for this one. The five years of night school made me a much more confident businessperson, and its completion felt worthy of a celebration. I stood in line, waiting to march into the auditorium, when the graduate in front of me began explaining that an MBA provided adequate qualifications to teach business courses at community colleges. Teaching had been on my mind, but I didn't realize I was qualified to do it. Being an adjunct professor seemed like it would make a great second career—instructing for a few hours a day and taking every summer off sounded a lot better than selling lockers. Anyway, because the MBA was complete, I was going to need a new project.

Shortly after graduation day, a building became available across the street from where I was renting warehouse space. I negotiated the price and accomplished the last goal I'd set for myself: own the building my company operated from and be its landlord. By that time, my nephew CJ had graduated from college and was working for my company. He started just as I had—on the day he completed his business degree. CJ had natural sales talent, great business sense, and was a lot more tech savvy than I was. He made a great addition to the company and started contributing immediately. I remembered how my father had allowed me to move forward with my ideas when I was CJ's age and how the company grew with my fresh energy. It became my turn to do the same. I'd crossed my self-imposed finish line in my endeavor in some respects—taking a start-up business from a dining room to a building

I owned—and found someone with tremendous ability who I could trust to run the business.

Time to slow down and focus on teaching.

I expected it to be an easy transition. With my experience and education, I was sure the community colleges would be fighting over me. Instead of rolling out the red carpet, though, my potential employers were silent. Instead of teaching, my new project was applying for teaching jobs. I sent hundreds of resumes with no responses, making me think I must have needed more credentials—so I enrolled at North Carolina State University for an online teaching certificate. The work in my locker company had become mundane to me. The building part I loved so much was complete, and it was a matter of maintaining what was already in place. By taking one class at a time, the teaching certificate took more than two years to finish, but I enjoyed the process and figured I'd be much more marketable as a teaching prospect with some actual credentials. I sent hundreds more resumes after I completed the certificate. Still, no response.

Many of the jobs I applied for required a doctorate, so I started to pursue one in business at an online university. It only took me about half of the first class to realize the course content was nowhere close to doctorate level, and there was no way a degree from the online university would mean anything to any educator I might encounter. Instead, I learned that Harvard University had an online extension course that included a marketing management certificate. Marketing was my forte, and because I was lacking the eighteen hours of graduate work many of the jobs required, I spent the next two-and-a-half years completing the Harvard certificate. That was a rewarding experience and included a weekend trip to Cambridge to learn marketing with the Ivy League types.

Certainly, this is all I could possibly need to finally land that elusive teaching job.

Months passed. I'd been checking every available job board and was unsuccessfully applying for adjunct teaching positions at learning institutions of every shape and size in a three-state radius. The importance of not quitting had been instilled in me long ago, so that was not an option. I knew what I wanted, and I was either going to get a job as an instructor or age out of the applicant pool. One Saturday morning, I was searching through my usual job sources when I noticed an opening for an adjunct entrepreneurship instructor advertised by a nearby community college.

The job ad was worded simply: "Recruitment for part-time instructor to deliver entrepreneurship program featuring business planning to a group of students in a minimum-security correctional setting."

Among the hundreds of applications, I'd applied for that exact opening about six months earlier. I remembered it because I was sure I'd be interviewed for the job. The only prerequisite for it was a bachelor's degree in any business field and a vague "some business experience preferred."

I've got that in spades.

The last page of the online application asked for a description of my teaching philosophy. Six months earlier, when I originally applied for the job, I filled that box with flowery maxims, such as "engage the learner" and "make it relevant," educational concepts I'd learned while earning the teaching certificate. The years of frustration caught up with me that day, though, and I reasoned that my previous swanky answer had gotten me nowhere.

This time, I typed my answer in all caps. "THERE IS ABSOLUTELY NO REASON FOR YOU TO NOT INTERVIEW ME FOR THIS POSITION. I HAVE ALL THE EDUCATION AND EXPERIENCE YOU COULD POSSIBLY ASK FOR, AND IF GIVEN THIS OPPORTUNITY, I WILL PUT THE SAME EFFORT INTO TEACHING THIS CLASS AS I DID WHILE TURNING MY

START-UP BUSINESS INTO A CONSISTENT LEADER IN MY INDUSTRY."

I figured my direct answer would quickly extinguish any consideration, but it felt good to write it. Two days later, however, my phone rang, and the woman on the other end identified herself as Sarah Shelton, the director of business technology and training at the community college I applied to. She asked if I was available to interview for the entrepreneurship instructor job at the prison.

Unbelievable! All I had to do this whole time was just get their attention.

Years of frustration had finally produced something tangible. I was so excited for my upcoming job interview that I went out and bought a new sports jacket and tie. I read everything I could about teaching in prison and learned as much as I could about the programs offered at the community college. I listened to numerous podcasts about interviewing skills and practiced answers to routine interview questions. I studied every book I could find on creating business plans. When the day arrived, I was as ready as I could possibly be.

CHAPTER FIVE

The Challenge Begins

"Whatever your hand finds to do, do it with all your might ..." —Ecclesiastes 9:10 (NIV)

MY DOGGED PURSUIT OF AN adjunct teaching position had taken me inside a prison and provided a brief glimpse of what life was like for an incarcerated felon. That world was so foreign to me that it had been difficult to comprehend in the short time I was there. Despite my reservations regarding my safety, I drove away from the prison feeling great about the interview. My career in sales gave me good people-reading skills, and I was nearly certain the job was mine. Nobody had said anything to make it official, but Richard writing me into the schedule sent a strong message.

I excitedly called my wife on the drive back home. "Guess who got a teaching job today?"

From the day I wanted to be a teacher some eight years ago, Reba had shared the experience with me. She stood by my side through the difficult MBA night classes, the years of formal online education, and the many struggles, challenges, and disappointments along the way. She shared my optimism as I slowly built a decent resume and the frustration of my long and fruitless job search. She was the one person who knew how passionately I had pursued a teaching job and was as excited as I was over the news.

"The classroom's not much," I explained. "I've got zero material to work with, no internet access, and I've got to deliver nine hours of content every week for eleven weeks starting next Thursday. Other than that, it's all good."

Reba wasn't going to let my challenge ahead put a damper on the moment.

"You did it," she said. "I'm so proud of you."

As I watched the rural homes and farms slowly turn into the asphalt and sprawl of my hometown, some trepidation eroded my elated feeling of accomplishment. It sure looked like I had class starting in less than two weeks—a class in which the only teaching aids were a crooked marker board and a Dave Ramsey book. What was I going to do?

The next morning, I sent a thank-you email to Sarah for the time interviewing me and for considering me for the position. Five minutes later, I received a return email officially offering me the job. It was a done deal. I quickly accepted, and she forwarded payroll forms, stating I'd have to attend a short orientation at the prison and have my background checked before I could start. For orientation, I was to report to the programs office and meet with Frank, the angry-looking Mr. Clean from my interview.

The next trip to the prison was a lot more enjoyable. I was no longer just a potential teacher; I was the new instructor! I arrived early and, that time, went through the guardhouse. The guard on duty called down to the programs office, verified my appointment, and pointed me toward the door to the prison yard. But after walking across the yard alone, I found the door locked. I knocked on the green metal and waited until a portly man in civilian clothes opened it with a confused look. After telling him why I was there, he silently pointed me toward Mr. Clean's office. He had a visitor ahead of me, so I stood outside his office, waiting for him to finish discussing a problem an inmate was having with a situation at home. When finished, Mr. Clean called me in with a stoic "I'm ready for you." His desk was so far forward in the small rectangular office, there was barely room for a chair—much less a chair with a person in it—between the front of his desk and the wall. I slid into the seat and sat with my legs sideways.

Mr. Clean's desk faced the door with a large computer screen separating him from whoever was sitting in the visitor's chair, making it difficult for me to see anything but the top of his shiny, bald head. His office was filled with small, cheeky, work-related statements. Next to the enormous silver-and-black "Big Bubba" insulated coffee mug on his desk was a wooden "Welcome to Camp Quitcherbitchin" sign. Hanging on the wall by the door were an array of similar signs, including one that said, "Notice: I'm not arguing, I'm just explaining why I'm right."

Mr. Clean requested my driver's license and asked, "Anything I should know about?" with inquisitive and somewhat accusatory eyes.

I suddenly realized I was in the hot seat of the prison.

"No sir," I replied as innocently as possible, silently wondering how many men had sat in this chair and spilled their guts. Mr. Clean went silent and started slowly tapping the keys on his keyboard. After a few minutes, he lifted his head to peek at me over the enormous monitor as if to give me a final opportunity to confess my sins before he found out anyway. I'd wondered over the years if some of my past transgressions had been what kept me from a teaching job. I had a DUI from my youth and was arrested for damage to property one night in the late 1980s, but that was a case of mistaken identity. I got an uneasy feeling, thinking that either offense could pop up on Mr. Clean's computer and end my teaching career before it started. The longer the process went, though, the more I started feeling like maybe it was all a bluff, so I sat silently for the next ten minutes, waiting for Mr. Clean to pronounce my sentence. He never said a word.

Once he slid my license back to me and began explaining the prison rules, I figured I was in.

In a monotonous voice, Mr. Clean explained the prison policies in simple terms. "No phones are allowed in here. If you bring a phone in, you don't work here anymore. No tobacco either. You'll be in less trouble for bringing marijuana in than if you bring tobacco, and if you smoke, you don't smoke on prison property. That includes smoking in your car if it's on prison property." The banal tone made it obvious he'd given this speech before.

"All you're allowed to provide the inmates with is classroom materials, which must all be returned to you at the end of class. Don't give them anything they aren't supposed to have. They like to start by asking for small favors, and once you've done something you weren't supposed to do, they'll use that to get bigger things."

The instructions made me feel like I was about to be turned loose in the lion's den. Mr. Clean went on to tell me about a guard who was caught smoking a cigarette by an inmate, and in exchange for not telling on him, the guard provided the inmate with a cigarette, which led to packs of cigarettes, eventually leading to cartons of cigarettes.

He continued. "Don't provide any personal information to any inmates. I had to let an officer go last week because she sent one of them a Bible through the mail, and the box had her home address on it. She was a good officer, but she broke the rules, so she gave me no choice."

I nodded obediently to all the instructions.

"We also have a zero-tolerance policy toward sexual harassment," Mr. Clean droned on. "I tell you this because this is a scenario that could happen. Let's say you have an inmate who hangs around after class and tells you he's worried about going back to his dorm because he thinks he might be sexually assaulted. It's your job to go immediately to the acting sergeant and report this to him. Do you remember where the sergeant's office is?"

"Sure," I said. "The place with the bathroom."

Mr. Clean winced at my lighthearted answer. "Let's say you don't report this immediately, and the inmate goes back to his dorm and *is* sexually assaulted. If we find out you knew about this attack before it took place and didn't do anything, *you* will be charged with a felony. That's how it works."

Great policy. The inmates have the ability to make me one of them.

Frank pressed on. "When you came for your interview the other day, you parked in our paved parking lot, but from now on, you'll park in the gravel lot by the front gate."

This meant I would have to go through the guardhouse every morning to be searched and walk the length of the whole prison yard to get to the dayroom in G Dorm. Mr. Clean wanted the guards to get to know me and assured me I'd eventually receive a key to the programs office, which would mean I could then park on the pavement and have access to the prison via a back gate. The programs office had a bathroom and hot coffee and was situated across the basketball court from G Dorm, providing much easier access to my classroom. Mr. Clean also said I'd be given the password to the computer in the programs office so I could use it during breaks.

He asked if I had any questions. I'd heard enough.

That began my rather precarious relationship with the prison staff. Since I was hired and paid by the local community college and didn't work directly for the prison, I was an outsider to the people who worked there. I was only there two days a week, keeping me out of the day-to-day drama and the office politics I'm sure played a big role in working there. The biggest difference between me and the staff, I'd learn, was in how we viewed the inmates. I'd been hired to teach principles of entrepreneurship, and I knew firsthand that starting a successful small business was one of the most difficult endeavors anyone could undertake. The failure rate of start-ups is staggering—nine out of ten fail.[1] In order for me to make my students believe they could someday start their own business, I knew I first had to get them to believe in themselves.

My objective to instill self-confidence in my students was the exact opposite goal of the people running the prison. Keeping everyone in line was an easier task when they were viewed as objects and not people. That level of dehumanization eliminated any favoritism with the inmates, which would likely lead to a disorderly prison.

Although the people who worked there might've thought I was wasting my time, they were almost always courteous to me. I got to know some of them on a first-name basis and made small talk with them on my way in and out of the guardhouse. I respected their authority; they didn't have an easy job and weren't paid much for doing it. At the same time, I kept my distance from them as much as possible. We were in opposite philosophical camps, and they had the power to disrupt everything I was trying so hard to accomplish.

* * *

Sarah gracefully granted me an extra week to prepare for my class, so I spent the next two weeks furiously compiling information on teaching entrepreneurship, using every source I could think of: books, podcasts, YouTube videos, and online articles. I dug in with both hands, digging as deep as I could muster. My best find was the book *Who Owns the Ice House?*, a true story narrated by an elderly man who learned entrepreneurship from his uncle back in the 1950s in Glen Allen, Mississippi. Uncle Cleve refused to work in the cotton fields like most of the people did in that time and place and instead bought the local ice house, which served as a platform to teach his young nephew the principles of entrepreneurship and how to be his own man. *Who Owns the Ice House?* was an excellent aid for teaching entrepreneurship, and it instantly became the backbone of my class plan. The book was divided into eight chapters covering different entrepreneurship principles, so each became a course topic in my syllabus—choice, opportunity, action, knowledge, wealth, brand, community, and persistence. I would cite them in order and apply them to similar business principles I'd learned in real life and studied in graduate school.

I found a business plan template and constructed it in the order of the topics. The plan would start with a feasibility blueprint and follow with a business profile, a business model, the business structure, risk management, money management, sales and marketing, and, finally, an executive summary. It was around fifteen pages. I decided to hand out the pages one at a time as the class progressed and have each student fill in the blanks for their unique business and the respective topic. They'd turn in the handwritten pages at the end of the week so I could type what they wrote over the following weekend and return it with the blank pages for the next topic. In eleven weeks, each student should build a nicely structured and professional-looking business plan tailored to whatever business they wanted to start. Typing all those pages for each business plan would be a lot of work for me, but the prison had no word processors or typewriters, and I could think of no other way to make it happen.

I remembered angry Mr. Clean's clear instructions to not give my students anything that I didn't collect at the end of class, but I was so eager to create a quality learning experience for my students, I decided to do it my way until I was told otherwise. I ordered enough *Ice House* books for everyone to have one and decided to spend the first week on choice, which was the title of chapter one. I thought it was a perfect starting point because making the choice to start a business was the biggest hurdle of all. If I couldn't convince my students it was a decision worthy of their consideration, the rest of the class wouldn't matter much. My students had all made choices that led them to a prison sentence, a common ground for everyone that would provide a firm foundation on which the classroom instruction could be built.

I found an organization based in eastern North Carolina, whose sole purpose was to prepare ex-offenders for a life of entrepreneurship. It was staffed by volunteers who had done prison time and were now running successful small businesses. The best part was that the program could provide guest speakers, so I was quick to put in a speaker request.

It should be powerful for the guys to see someone who's been where they are and got out and actually made it happen. Also, it'll fill an entire class.

I spent just about every available waking hour before my first class trying to come up with enough material to fill the first nine hours.

If I can stay one week ahead, I might just pull this off.

My optimism faded a bit when the first *Ice House* books arrived. On the cover was an aging Black man wearing overalls and standing alone in a cotton field. I wasn't sure how the stereotypical and dated-looking cover would resonate with my primarily Black students. If they were anything like the guys I'd seen in the prison yard, it might not go over well.

You might as well put Aunt Jemima on there for good measure.

Borrowing heavily from the style of Dr. Erevelles, I decided to incorporate as much hands-on and interactive material as I could find. From my sales background, I knew the importance of a good first impression and tried to find something that would wow the students and show that the class would be different from others they'd taken.

I found what I thought would be a great way to start my first class from the website of an entrepreneurship instructor. In order to illustrate how entrepreneurship differed from working for someone else, the instructor first divided the class into two groups. The first group was given a standard jigsaw puzzle and told to put the puzzle together. The second group was given a set of random-colored magnets and given the same instruction. When each group had completed their puzzle, they switched.

What a great way to illustrate that entrepreneurship has no set of instructions to go by and no preordained finish.

I knew the exercise would get my first class engaged immediately, give them the opportunity to work together, and take up at least an hour of classroom time. I had material for my first week of teaching and was ready to go.

Or so I thought.

CHAPTER SIX
You Gotta Start Somewhere

"Every new experience brings its own maturity and a greater clarity of vision."
—Indira Gandhi, former prime minister of India

IT WAS A BEAUTIFUL, COOL, clear spring morning when I pulled into the prison to start my teaching career. I parked in the gravel lot as instructed and walked to the tiny guardhouse that served as a buffer between the prison and the outside world. I had a large gym bag filled with books, notebooks, pens, and handouts. I walked into the guardhouse through a silent metal detector and was greeted by a slender guard in his midsixties. His pockmarked face studied me behind Coke-bottle-thick glasses.

"Wacha got in dere?" he asked in a thick-as-molasses country accent, nodding toward my gym bag.

I unzipped the bag and stood back as he slowly dug through it. He went straight to the pieces of my magnet puzzle, which I'd placed on top of my other material in a clear Ziploc bag.

He took an immediate interest in the contents and studied me, cynically asking, "Waas all dis?"

I made an effort to explain why I needed a magnetic puzzle but only got a few words out before he cut me off, removing the baggie as he spoke.

"You can't bring no magnets in here. They'll use them to hide stuff. I'll give this back to you on your way out." Satisfied he'd done his job, he abandoned his bag search and waved me toward the door leading to the yard.

So much for my big opening. I made my way through the empty prison yard to the dayroom of G Dorm and waited for my first students to arrive.

"Code two, count is clear," The twangy Southern accent crackled over the tiny speaker anchored in the corner of the empty dayroom. "Get off your bunks. The yard is closed. No inmates are allowed back in the dorms 'til 11 a.m."

Low but steady snores reverberated from the adjoining bunk room where thirty or so men slept in tiny metal bunkbeds.

I guess that doesn't apply to them.

The door to the dayroom had a large window on its upper half. Soon, a stocky Black man with a huge, knitted black Rastafarian hat hanging halfway down his back stared at me through the window, opened the door, and strode confidently to a table in the front row. Without making eye contact, he sat down and stared at the wall in front of him. A slim, middle-aged Black man followed him in, giving me a closed-mouth smile and choosing a seat at the table closest to the door. Next through the door was an older Black man with a weak eye who, after a brief discussion, took the seat the slim man had chosen, sending him sheepishly to another table. Next to arrive was a stocky white man with a crew cut who appeared to be in his early forties.

"I transferred from another camp to take this class, so I hope it's worth it," he told me, taking a seat front and center. Five more inmates eventually trickled through the door, each dressed in prison-issued army-green pants and heather-gray T-shirts. Some wore dark-green yard jackets with large front pockets. The last to arrive was a light-skinned Black man with a thin Afro. He wore Clark Kent-style glasses and a bemused smile.

Here goes nothing.

My eight-year ambition to teach in a classroom had finally come to fruition, but with my puzzle confiscated, I wasn't 100 percent sure where to start. I walked up to the crooked white-board, and so began my formal teaching career.

"My name is John McLaughlin," I told them. "But that's a difficult name to remember and even more difficult to write, so how about everyone calls me Moose?"

While saying this, I wrote *MOOSE* in big blue letters on the whiteboard. Moose was a nickname I somehow gained many years ago from the character Mr. Moose on *Captain Kangaroo*. I'd decided to use a moniker for two reasons: it would be easier for the inmates to remember and pronounce "Moose" than my last name, and it would provide a cloak of anonymity. At the time, I didn't want any students to look me up when they got out.

I didn't realize all staff in the prison were automatically referred to as "Mr." or "Ms.," so although it wasn't exactly what I'd planned, I was known from that day forward as "Mr. Moose."

"I've never taught a class before," I told them. "And I've never been in a prison before, so it's safe to say I'm going to learn a lot more from you over the next eleven weeks than you could possibly learn from me."

The inmates exchanged looks of bewilderment. What I didn't realize at that moment was that my time in prison was going to dismantle a lot of stereotypes for both me and my students. Any notions my students might've had that teachers were know-it-alls who focused on delivering lessons they'd later test on for the sole purpose of assigning a letter grade would soon, hopefully, be eradicated. Likewise, my preconceived notion of prison inmates as lost causes who were getting the punishment they deserved would also soon be radically changed.

"Let's start with the rules of my class." I continued. "You don't have to agree with someone else's opinion, but you do have to respect it. And while we're on the topic of respect, when someone else is talking, they have the floor. I don't want any side conversations. If you've got something to say, share it with all of us. We all come from different places and have different experiences, so this class is going to be a lot better if we can all learn from each other. If you want to just sit there and listen to what I've got to say, it won't be nearly as good of a class, and you won't learn as much as you would if everyone contributes." I handed each inmate an eighty-page bound notebook—no wire, per prison policy—with a sticker bearing the class logo I'd created. It was a large equilateral triangle with words on each of the three points. "Sales" was emblazoned at the top point, the lower left point said "Hard Work & Discipline," and the lower right point read "Money Management." I explained to the class and all those who would follow that the logo was my holy trinity of entrepreneurship. You had to be capable in all three areas to succeed.

"I'm providing everyone with a notebook and a pen, but take care of it," I explained. "They don't give me any money for supplies to teach this class, so anything you get, I had to pay for from my own pocket. These notebooks provide you with a place to write things down. You never know when someone's going to say something worth remembering, and don't expect it to always be me."

I then handed everyone a copy of *Who Owns the Ice House?* and explained that because I'd paid for the books myself, they were free to write in and keep them.

"This isn't property of the prison," I told them. "This belongs to you."

The students seemed appreciative, especially after I explained I'd paid for the materials myself.

I began a mini-review of the class and explained we'd read each chapter of the book in order, giving them the assignment of reading the first chapter before our 8:00 a.m. meeting the next day.

"Everyone in this class is going to have the opportunity to create a business plan they can use when they get out of here. Every plan will be different because every business is different. But in order to write a plan, you've got to first think of a business to run after you're released, so that'll be our first step. Most of us will start service businesses because we can start these with very little money. Service businesses are sometimes referred to as blue-collar businesses, so let's take a look at the biggest of these in terms of sales dollars as of last year." I went to the board and wrote down "Construction," along with the sales figures for 2016. I took a quick peek at the class and noticed a few students had opened their notebooks and were writing.

Son of a gun. I'm teaching!

My classes convened Thursday and Friday mornings, and the same group of students met Monday through Wednesday every week for the commercial cleaning part of the class, which Richard taught.

The prison staff "counted" the inmates four times a day. During the head count, the inmates had to stay where they were, typically on their bunks, until everyone was accounted for and the count "cleared." If the number of inmates counted didn't match the number that were supposed to be at the camp, the count was done again, as many times as was necessary to ensure that no inmate had escaped. The morning count was typically complete around 8:00 a.m., after which the inmates would be instructed over the PA system to leave their bunks and clean the prison yard. Once the count was cleared, my students would start arriving in G Dorm for class. Classes were sometimes delayed until the guards could get the count right. I had waits of up to forty-five minutes on days when they were unable to account for all the inmates. The unexpected delays would disrupt my teaching plan for the day, but I learned delays were part of the experience.

I learned Richard's class would take a break at 9:30 a.m., which seemed like a logical time for everyone to get up and refresh themselves for ten minutes, so I instituted a 9:30 a.m. break for my classes as well. G Dorm was near the programs office, and if a staff member was in there, I could be let in to use the bathroom or make copies. If no one was in, the next facility available to me was in the sergeant's office at the other end of the camp.

I was on my way to the programs office during the break in my first class when a stocky young Black inmate stopped me. He wore thick black glasses, knew my name, and wanted to know if I could spare any *Ice House* books. The guys in my class had barely had time to get out the door for their first break, and I was incredulous that I'd already encountered an inmate who knew my name and the book I was giving out.

Amazing how fast word travels in this place.

"Thank you, Mr. Moose," he said with an ear-to-ear grin after I handed him a spare book. It was the first of many books I handed out to someone not registered for my class. Even though I wasn't given any funds for supplies, I couldn't deny an incarcerated man a book on my first day, my last day, or any day in between. I could usually find a used copy, so the cost was manageable, and I could think of no better resource for someone who wanted information in an effort to improve themselves and had the time to do so.

I continued across the concrete basketball court to the programs office roughly thirty feet from G Dorm. An enormous inmate, easily 350 pounds, stopped me and asked if I was the new entrepreneurship teacher. He looked like he could lift the entire G Dorm if he wanted to. He had a scar running from the corner of his mouth to his neck, a shiny bald head, sunglasses, and an over-the-top jolly disposition.

"I'm an entrepreneur," he explained. "I'm writing a book." He then launched into an impromptu rhyming story, almost a rap, that started with me waking up to a phone call and ended with the two of us going on a trip to Atlanta to make some sort of business deal. The huge guy had a knack for rhyming and storytelling, and I liked him right away. He introduced himself as Sampson and asked if he could sit in on my class.

"Why don't you register for it?" I asked.

He looked at me with a shy grin and explained he had a life sentence with no parole, and they didn't let people without an exit date take classes.

"You're more than welcome in my class," I told him. "We need as many entrepreneurs in there as we can get." I meant it, too. From my first impression, he could've taken the place of two or three guys who looked like they didn't want to be there. It couldn't hurt to have what was likely the biggest guy in the prison on my side either.

Sampson followed me in after the break and became a staple in that class and all of the classes that followed for over a year, until eventually he was transferred for some sort of disagreement with another inmate, which I never fully understood. Sampson always sat in the middle of the room and made great contributions. He was usually in good spirits—although sometimes strangely sullen—and he worked hard on an array of business plans that usually didn't get past the first page or two.

I somehow made it through my first class and spent the afternoon at my locker company in Charlotte, which got me home around 6:30 p.m. It didn't seem like a long time before I was back in the car Friday morning and heading toward the prison. My second time through the guardhouse went a lot more smoothly. I told the aging guard I didn't bring any "funny stuff," and that seemed to be good enough for him. He waved me right through the gate.

I left the guardhouse and was heading toward G Dorm when an inmate stopped me, glaring directly into my eyes.

"Are you the new business teacher?" he asked. He was a thirty-something Black man who kept his hair cut close to his scalp and had the physique of a well-trained cruiserweight boxer. He was intimidating, and there was something about the way he approached me that seemed aggressive. He didn't smile and didn't break eye contact. It was uncomfortable for me to be in his presence, and I felt like he was trying to decide whether to trust me or kick my ass right there in the prison yard.

"Yes, I am," I said, trying to look confident.

"I'm writing a book," he said, still staring at me. "It's a self-help book. Do you think that's a good idea?"

My sigh of relief was enormous. "I think that's a great idea," I said.

"If I come by your classroom later, could you look it over for me?" he asked.

"Absolutely!" I said, grateful he was asking for help and not looking to hurt me.

He stopped by later that day, introducing himself as Josh while he showed me the outline for his book. He planned to dedicate each chapter to a charitable cause and compare the disease or problem the cause stood for to a personal problem that needed to be overcome by the reader. For example, chapter three might be sponsored by the American Cancer Society, and it would entail how unresolved issues in your psyche could act as a cancer in your life.

"Do you think these charities would let me use their logos?" Josh asked.

"I think so," I said. "As long as you cut them in on the profits, I don't see why they wouldn't."

My answer got the first smile out of Josh. What I'd originally taken for aggression was raw determination. I got to know him well in the time he had remaining in prison, typed up a few business plans for him, and shared some information on publishing when he asked for it.

The guys I got to know well sometimes shared their release dates with me, and I could usually remember how much time each of them had left within a day or two. For Josh, it was nine months from when I met him. I had the good fortune of seeing him in the yard the day before he was released. He looked like a new person, relaxed and smiling, a totally different disposition from the first time I met him.

"You made it," I told him. "I can't wait to see what you do with the rest of your life."

What Josh did was pretty amazing. He wrote and published his first book, started a trucking business, traveled the country giving motivational speeches and founded an organization that teaches the principles of financial literacy and entrepreneurship to inmates and people in underserved communities. Years after we first met in the prison yard, I bought twenty copies of his book for the prison library and used them in the classes I taught.

CHAPTER SEVEN
Learning to Teach

"When one teaches, two learn."
—Robert Heinlein, American author

MY SECOND DAY AS AN instructor taught me that I had a lot to learn to be effective.

I thought I'd start with a review of chapter one from *Ice House*.

"Did everyone read chapter one as assigned?" I asked.

A few guys made an effort to get their book out. Everyone else tried very hard not to make eye contact. I gave a brief summary of the chapter and asked if anyone had anything they'd like to add. Total silence. I put the book down and tried to figure out what to talk about next.

"That's it?" the light-skinned man I later learned was named Kevin asked. "That's all you're going to say?"

He's right. That was really thin.

"Let me ask you something," Kevin said. Even though it was only our second meeting, most students had made some sort of contribution by now. That was the first time Kevin had spoken up. "If this is a true story, do you think Uncle Cleve could've been a part of Black Wall Street? The time period's about right, and he had to learn those business skills somewhere."

I had no idea what he was talking about. “What was Black Wall Street?” I asked.

“Black Wall Street!” Kevin continued, slightly exasperated and looking around the room for support. “Look it up. An affluent Black community in Oklahoma around the turn of the century that was bombed out of existence by the United States Army.”

I gave him and the rest of the class a reminder. “Just like I said on day one, I’m going to learn a whole lot more from you than you could ever learn from me.”

I took two things away from that interaction: I had to do a better job on chapter reviews, and I had to figure out what Kevin was talking about. Some weekend research about Black Wall Street revealed it was everything Kevin said, but not part of the standard history book—at least not the ones I’d read. I liked Kevin’s passion, though, and I learned a few weeks later he was a poet. He’d published some works online and in some prison publications. I read some of his poems and thought his writing was good. In one, he equated modern-day prisoners as slaves. I didn’t understand the correlation at the time, but it made a lot more sense as I got more familiar with the prison work release program months later.

After our morning break, I handed out an online article written by a man who had done some time in prison and discovered that his time spent learning how to survive in that environment helped him become a better entrepreneur. The article explained how the lack of control and resources in prison was similar to what a start-up entrepreneur encountered when building a business.

The class seemed unusually focused on the article, and Kevin, who was rightfully critical earlier, said “More stuff like this” after he finished reading it. It had to be obvious I was still finding my way as an instructor, so I appreciated the feedback.

After our morning break, I wanted to show a DVD. It was a lesson from a college professor who taught entrepreneurship that I planned on using throughout the course. The video lessons were thirty minutes each to help fill the class time, and I thought actual college material might reinforce some of the course principles I was less formally providing.

When the class returned, we walked over to the chapel and crammed into the side-pocket meeting room where I'd been interviewed. The small room with the oversized conference table could barely hold the ten guys, and it proved inefficient to leave G Dorm, walk across the basketball court to the chapel, set up, then come back and try to pick back up in the dayroom. One student wandered away from the group on the trip back and didn't return for the day. That was the first and last class that went to the chapel for a DVD presentation. For the sake of consistency, I knew I had to figure out a way to keep everyone together in the same room.

I had a small DVD player with a USB port at home that my wife and I would sometimes take on our excursions so we could watch movies in hotel rooms. I'd never make it through the long classes with only a whiteboard and a Dave Ramsey book, and I couldn't keep showing movies in a different part of the prison, so I spent the next weekend figuring out how to show slides from the DVD player. I finally figured out that by saving a PowerPoint presentation in JPEG format, the player could read the slides. The only trick was that it automatically forwarded through them, so I learned to keep the DVD on pause and carefully advance the slides one at a time. It was a step in the right direction because by incorporating the DVD player, I could not only show DVDs, I could incorporate the slides I'd used for presentations in my MBA program and create new presentations on the topics I wanted to cover. I felt confident the long classes would be a lot more interesting with these new teaching aids.

The two small TVs attached to the wall in G Dorm were at my disposal. They were spread apart so two different channels could be shown. The volume was always off; the inmates would listen to whatever channel was on via their clear transistor radios. Because I was only able to connect my DVD player to one small TV and one TV would be difficult for the whole room to view, using my own TV seemed like a better solution. I had a large one at work we weren't using, so I figured I'd take it in, put it in the center of the classroom, and leave it in the programs office after class. Knowing it would take more than one trip from my car to the classroom, I arrived extra early the next Thursday.

The same old guard who'd confiscated my magnets the week before quickly foiled the plan. He saw me walking across the gravel parking lot carrying the big flat-screen TV and stood up from his small desk, ready for me as soon as I opened the door.

"You can't bring that in here!" he barked when I was halfway through the door.

"What's wrong with a TV?" I asked. "We've got two of them in my classroom already."

"'Cause you can't, that's why," the guard shot back with a defiant look.

"I'm going to keep it in the programs office when I'm not using it, so it'll be controlled the whole time," I explained.

"Not going to happen. You got to leave it with me," he said, unwavering.

Not wanting to give him the satisfaction of holding my TV, I took it back to the car and got my book bags.

Looks like plan B.

The second time through the guardhouse, the old guy just waved me in with a stern warning. "This is a prison. You can't just bring anything you want in here."

That geezer was becoming quite an obstacle to my early

teaching attempts. I sure wasn't going to tell him I had a DVD player in my book bag.

Left with no other choice, it was then a matter of hooking my DVD player to one of the TVs. I arrived at G Dorm to an empty dayroom. Count had not yet cleared, giving me time to investigate the setup. I had my rig ready; it was just a matter of getting the TV off the wall, connecting the RCA cord, and placing it back on the wall.

This being a prison, I wasn't sure if extra measures had been taken to secure things like TVs to walls. If so, I'd need some help from the staff getting everything hooked up, but I'd learned firsthand that they were there mostly to deter my progress.

I had the RCA cord on a splice, so I'd only have to connect it once. Then, I could hide the cord when I left for the day, and no one would be the wiser. Although I'd installed one once, I wasn't too familiar with TV brackets. I lucked out, though, as that one seemed to be like all the others: two cords hanging down beneath the TV, which, when pulled, would release the set.

By that time, one of my students, Darius, had made it to class, so I asked him for his assistance. Darius was a young, lanky African American with long dreadlocks and a big smile. He sat at the front table with the stocky white guy with the crew cut and, from what I could tell, was enjoying my class.

Darius hesitated at first. "You know they're watching us, right?" he asked, nodding at one of the security cameras mounted in the corner of the ceiling.

"Come on, Darius. This is in the interest of higher education," I urged.

Darius flashed me his million-dollar smile and said, "Well, if you put it that way."

I instructed him to pull on the cords while I pulled the TV off the wall.

"I'm glad to be doing this with you and not another guy in a prison uniform," Darius said quietly.

In no time, I had my rig connected to the TV and the TV back in place. Our entire clandestine operation took less than three minutes, and by that time, most of the class had arrived and taken a keen interest in what Darius and I were up to.

I hooked up the rig and put in a twenty-minute YouTube video about an ex-offender who started a successful yoga studio after his release from prison.

After my video was over, I announced, "In case any of you are wondering, we won't be watching movies in the chapel anymore. We'll be staying in our classroom."

It seemed like a great moment in my early teaching career. I had a way to show video content without leaving G Dorm, and I'd done it using my own ideas without permission from anyone. But I wasn't going to be the instructor who let the movies do the teaching, so the next step was to see if I could get my slides working. I had an old PowerPoint presentation I'd given to some undergraduate entrepreneurship classes years before that told the story of how my dad and I started a business together, the obstacles we faced, how we overcame them, and what the small business we started had become. I put the jump drive in the USB port on the front of the DVD player and hoped it would work as well as it had at home. Success!

In one of the early slides, I had a picture of my dad handing me the first check I earned working for him way back in 1987. It was my mom's idea to take the picture, and I'd found it when I originally made the presentation years earlier.

Some of the guys in the back were struggling to view the tiny TV screen, but they all took notice when that slide came on.

"That's you, Mr. Moose?" one of them asked, referring to the smiling twenty-three-year-old kid holding his first paycheck like he'd just won the lottery. The older inmate with the lazy eye got out of his chair at the back of the room and walked halfway to the front of the class to get a better look.

"Running your own business for thirty years will sure as heck turn your hair gray," I explained as he strained to see the screen.

"How much is that check for?" he asked.

"I was paid $600 twice a month, and each check netted to $480.50 after taxes." I remembered the amount because I'd received that exact sum for years. "That's $14,400 annually, which kept me well below the poverty line."

"That's good money," the old man said, in no way sarcastically, as he shuffled back toward his table by the door. At first, I thought his comment was meant to be funny, but he didn't look like the type of guy who would make a quip like that. I started to wonder if the gulf between my life experiences and those of some of my students might be too big for us to find much common ground.

In two weeks, I'd gone from a crooked whiteboard and a Dave Ramsey book to a classroom with video content and slideshows. The guys noticed the effort I put forth and began to realize I had no ulterior motives except to try to help them. We were slowly starting to build a level of trust with each other. I was having so much fun finally being a teacher that my excitement became contagious. They seemed like a different group of guys than the stone-faced inmates I started with two weeks earlier.

I dismissed the class at the end of my second week with instructions to read chapter two of *Who Owns the Ice House?*

and was packing up my things when I noticed the stocky white man with the crew cut had decided to stay seated. Jack had been paying full attention to my class material up to that point and had been studying me curiously. He strode up to my table as I packed up my files and the DVD player.

"Why are you doing this?" he asked point-blank in his gravelly voice.

"Teaching is something I've always wanted to do, and this is the only job I could get," I answered.

Jack appeared to accept my answer, but he looked at me in a way that made me realize I was operating in very unfamiliar surroundings.

"I like what you're doing," he said flatly. "But you can't just let anybody wander in here and sit in on your class. You need to get permission for him." He nodded toward Sampson, who'd also remained behind and was sitting at his table furiously writing in his notebook, completely oblivious to our conversation.

"Permission from whom?" I asked.

"Kemper, the head of programs."

I thanked Jack as he turned to leave. He was trying to keep me out of trouble, but that meant another meeting with Mr. Clean, and I couldn't see anything good coming out of it.

Because I didn't want to make a big mistake right out of the gate, I made one of my few ventures into the office of the head of programs after my next class. I asked about getting a key so I could use the bathroom when I needed to and if it would be okay to let an unregistered student sit in during class time. Mr. Clean ignored my request for a key but took a keen interest in who I might be letting in my class.

He peeked over his computer monitor with his typical pained expression. "Who?" he asked.

"Sampson," I answered.

With an instant look of bemusement, he replied, "Sure. Sampson is fine."

I thanked him and made a quick exit. I'd gotten what I wanted and didn't see any sense in sticking around.

That established my open-door policy for my entrepreneurship class—anyone who wanted to learn was always welcome. Whenever a new face appeared, he would typically hesitate by the door and gauge my reaction, then find a place to sit along the back wall. I would stop whatever I was doing, grab a pen and a notebook with the class logo, and walk back and hand it to them while asking their name. I always thanked them for coming and got back to the subject at hand. It didn't take much to make the guys feel welcome. Before long, I was buying notebooks and pens by the case.

By the time I started my class on Thursdays, my registered students had spent three days together and already developed a sort of classroom chemistry. When an unregistered inmate would ask a question or contribute, the registered students would sometimes get exasperated or put their heads on the desk. It was obvious not all of them liked having outsiders in their class or that I let the unregistered guys come and go as they pleased. (Some had other obligations at the prison and couldn't be there for the whole class.) No matter how unpopular it was, I wasn't going to turn away anyone who wanted to be there.

The guys who came in off the yard were frequently my best students. They often had business experience or questions and were there to learn things they could apply and better their lives. Those who formally took my class got twenty-seven days off their sentence, two nicely printed college certificates, and an all-day graduation party at the end of the class consisting of fried chicken, pizza, salad, dessert, and two movies. The guys who came in on their own accord usually got none of the above. I thought teaching them might be teaching in its purest form. There was no mandatory attendance, no letter grades, and the only reward they received was whatever they gained from my material.

I continued letting others into the class because I determined that if Sampson was okay, then everyone was okay, and I wasn't going to ask permission for anyone else. It was an environment where *no* seemed to be the favorite answer to my every question, and I figured it was a lot easier to ask for forgiveness rather than permission.

Sampson was a great student, and I enjoyed getting to know him. He came from eastern North Carolina and was almost always in a good mood. Despite his life sentence with no possibility of parole, he maintained a naive attitude that he would get off on a technicality and be set free. I learned he'd been in prison more than fifteen years for murder, an act he denied. Sampson explained that when he first came to prison, he was angry and got into a lot of trouble, but one day, he turned his life over to Jesus and had since led a clean life. When I met Sampson, he said he'd never agreed to the "life, no parole" plea bargain he was granted and had never signed anything.

"I wasn't there when that man was murdered," he explained. "And I didn't agree to any plea deal."

One day, Sampson brought in some papers he said consisted of his legal appeal. "This is the man who's going to get me out," he said, pointing to the law firm's letterhead. I was able to read a few words over his shoulder and picked up a few descriptive phrases, like "childlike" and "overly trusting"—both of which seemed to accurately describe the man I was getting to know.

Sampson had a great work ethic to go along with his entrepreneurial spirit. He'd already written at least two books, including a children's book, so I brought him information on how to self-publish. In prison, there were no word processors, cell phones were forbidden, and I never saw a typewriter. Like everyone else, he did all of his writing by hand.

One of his many business plans consisted of making wine because he'd learned in prison how to make some sort of fermented drink in a plastic garbage bag using tomatoes, sugar, and water—or whatever he could scrounge from the kitchen. His plan involved growing grapes and bottling quality wine like a real vintner, but I sort of liked the "ferment whatever you can find" plan better. I tried to convince Sampson we could come up with a kit that included everything needed to make prison hooch at home, including the plastic garbage bag, and we could write his story on the box we packaged it in. I could imagine college kids making the concoction and daring each other to drink it. Sampson never signed on with my plan, though. He wanted to make the good stuff.

"If it comes from the earth, it comes from God," he explained.

In a later class, Sampson decided he wanted to design clothing. "Everyone needs clothes," he said. "You can't come out of your house without clothes on, and sooner or later, you got to come out." Sampson snickered and grinned ear-to-ear. His biggest concern was designing a logo and getting his trademark registered. I worked with him for a few weeks on the logo. He wanted to incorporate his last name, which started with an *F* and the letter *W* for wear. He also wanted to include a heart with the logo to show he loved his customers. I brought in numerous fonts and heart symbols until he found what he liked, and I put it all together in a bright, clean logo he approved.

Sampson wasn't ready to start production until his logo was legally registered. He constantly worried someone was going to steal his trademark, and I spent a lot of time trying to explain how unnecessary it was to spend money registering it in the start-up phase of his business.

"We haven't sold anything yet," I tried to explain. "We've got nothing to protect."

Despite my advice, Sampson was convinced his design would be stolen and someone would profit off his creativity.

"If that happens," I told him repeatedly, "we still have legal rights. We can make them stop using it and take whatever money they've made from using it."

Sampson always eyed me skeptically during those conversations, but coming from his environment, I understood his concerns. After weeks of persuasion, I finally pushed Sampson over the trademark hurdle so that we could move forward with designing clothes.

"If somebody steals it, I'll just design another one," he finally reasoned.

Sampson came to my class the next week with a design he wanted to put on a hoodie. It was a set of praying hands and the words "Power of Prayer." I took it home and worked on his design and brought a few different versions of it for his approval. After a few weeks of going back and forth, I created something he liked.

"Now, we can move into production," I told him. "We've got to figure out how to sell these."

I found a website that would print on demand, but we would need to presell at least twelve hoodies to make a production run. Sampson set the price, and I sent a link to everyone I could think of that might take an interest in what he'd created.

My sales efforts failed miserably, and because I didn't have the heart to tell Sampson our sales were at zero, I decided to buy the minimum quantity of hoodies myself. I considered it part of my job to give my students some hope in their entrepreneurial efforts, and I thought if Sampson could actually see one of the hoodies he created, it might help him realize he really could be an entrepreneur, even while sitting in prison.

When the Power of Prayer hoodies arrived, I sent them to some of the people Sampson knew on the outside, including his wife. I thought it best to not bring a hoodie in to show him. I knew he'd want to keep it, and he was such a huge man that I didn't think there was any way I could physically take it away from him once he had it in his possession.

A few weeks later, Sampson took me aside and told me his wife had worn his Power of Prayer hoodie on a recent visiting day.

He said, "When I saw my design and logo on that hoodie, Mr. Moose, it gave me chills." His nostrils flared, and his eyes bugged at the memory. That was early in my prison teaching career, and I was unsure if I'd done the right thing with his hoodie. Did I give false hope to someone with a life sentence, or did I empower him?

After Sampson sat through three or four full-length courses, he'd learned all of my material and became the resident entrepreneurship expert. I could always count on him to speak up when I needed a contribution, and he always had a smile on his face.

Until one class. I'd put together a case study that told the story of some college students who were considering starting a paper shredding business. I instructed the class to read the study, and as a group, we tried to answer the questions that followed. The whole point of the exercise was to show the value of creating a business plan before starting a business. I used it right before we started our individual business plans in hopes of getting some buy-in from the group on what was ahead.

The class read the case study, and I started asking questions. First, how much should we charge our customers? Second, which of the three paper shredders should we buy? In my teaching, I was always quick to remind the students there were no right or wrong answers. Starting a business was not like solving a math problem. You never know what might work until you put the plan into action. I was getting nowhere with that class, though. No answers and lots of people looking down or out the windows.

After getting silence, in an act of complete desperation, I went to my whiteboard and asked in a raised voice, "Okay then, why don't we just buy the biggest paper shredder we can find, put it in the back of our pickup truck, and drive around town trying to find customers, letting them decide how much they want to pay us to shred their papers?"

No one made an attempt to answer at first. Then Sampson, who'd been through the case study with at least two other classes, stood up from his seat.

"I'll tell you why." I'd never seen Sampson angry before, but he looked extremely irritated by my question, and as he provided his answer, he started moving menacingly toward the front of the room where I was standing. "Because if we did all that like you said . . ." By that time, Sampson was clenching his fists and speaking through gritted teeth as he continued on his path toward me. He stopped about ten feet away, stared me straight in the eye, and announced in his loudest voice, "We'd be driving around in our truck with our paper shredder like a bunch of damn fools!"

I wasn't sure what was going to come next. There was no way I could make it to the door first if he decided to charge at me, and I was pretty sure I wouldn't get any help from anyone in the room if Sampson got violent.

"You're exactly right," I told him in the gentlest voice I could muster. "Thank you, Sampson."

He slowly turned around and walked back to his seat, staring angrily out the window for the next half hour. I never learned what brought on that radical personality change. I thought maybe the frustrated tone of my question had triggered an aggressive impulse, or maybe he was just as irritated as I was that no one was contributing or paying attention to our case study. I was careful from that point forward to keep my voice inflections in check.

One of the students in my first class was a tall young white man from the North Carolina mountains named Jacob. He had an arrogance about him I initially thought was out of place. He didn't contribute much until our third week when I called on the guys to find out if they had an idea for the type of business they wanted to start. Haughtily, Jacob told us he was a fully licensed air conditioning and furnace inspector, and his father ran a heating and air conditioning service in his hometown. Jacob had a job at his father's company waiting for him upon his release.

I did some research into the business and into competing air conditioning businesses in the small mountain community, then put together a presentation for the next class.

"Jacob is extremely lucky," I told the group. "Not only does he have a job waiting for him when he gets out, but he has the opportunity of a lifetime to take an existing small business to the next level." I began my presentation by showing slides of the websites of the three competing HVAC companies in Jacob's dad's target market. Jacob knew something about all of them and had even worked for one of them. Then, I got to his dad's business. "Your dad doesn't have a website," I pointed out.

"Nope," Jacob said. "He doesn't understand that kind of stuff."

"Neither does my dad," I explained. "That's why he needs you. I'll bet your dad works a fifty- to sixty-hour week and is great with his customers."

"He is," Jacob agreed.

"Just think how much more business a good website would bring in." I was excited for Jacob's situation. It was similar to what I'd been through with my business years before; I knew he was in the unique position to take a good company and make it better. "Once your father sees how much you can help his business, he's very likely to start turning day-to-day decisions over to you, and in a short period of time, you could be the owner-operator. I hope you see the opportunity that's right in front of you."

Jacob shared none of my enthusiasm for the bright future I'd painted for him. "Everybody up there knows what I did," he said. "How am I ever going to get them to give me a second chance? My dad's business has suffered a lot already because of me."

That caught me completely off guard, which happened often, especially in the early years. I had a tendency to occasionally forget we were sitting in a prison dayroom and not in a college classroom.

All I could think to say to Jacob was, "Not everyone is going to give you a second chance right away. You're going to have to prove yourself, and your actions are going to speak a lot louder than your words. I'd join a church or volunteer somewhere in the community and show the people there that you're a changed man. It won't be easy, and you're going to have to really want it, but I think you can earn that second chance if you work hard enough."

I had no idea what Jacob did to end up in prison, although it was easy to look my students up on the internet and find out. If you had a first and last name, there were numerous websites that would provide you with the crimes committed, the lengths of sentences, infractions committed in prison, and any other pertinent information. I'd promised myself not to do that when I accepted the job. I voiced to my students that I was teaching a class all about letting go of the past and focusing on the future, and I didn't want to violate my own principle by looking up their past sins behind their backs. If an inmate told me what he'd done, fine. If he didn't, I wanted to afford him his privacy. I made an exception with Jacob, however. I wanted to reinforce my second-chance plan with him and thought I would be on stronger ground if I knew what he did. What I learned was that Jacob was driving drunk one morning in his small community and hit a girl who was waiting for her school bus. I didn't read any more than that, so I never found out if she survived—the incident was too horrific—but I instantly understood Jacob's concern about getting a second chance.

After reading up on Jacob, I spent the next few hours looking for YouTube videos on regret and compassion. I found a TED Talk about regrets by journalist Kathryn Schulz, who used her poor decision to get a tattoo to illustrate the power of regret. She listed three principles of regret. First, regret is there for a reason. Second, the actions you regret are usually not as bad or as important to other people as you think. Third, you can't let regret rule your life. You need to learn from it and move forward.

While the situations were far from the same, I believed the general principles would be beneficial for everyone in the class to hear and I couldn't wait to get back to G Dorm to show it. By that time, I'd figured out how to splice the signal into the second small TV on the wall so everyone in the room had a better view of my videos and slides.

My teaching plan quickly took shape. I felt like I could find material relevant to not only the entrepreneurship part of the course, but also material that might help some of the guys move forward. I discovered a good way to start class was with a twenty-minute inspirational video because my students had to check in at the sergeant's office before coming, so they didn't all arrive at the same time. I usually didn't have a full class for at least ten minutes, so there was no point in starting with class-related material. A motivational video was a good way to wake everyone up, and the guys seemed to like them.

From what I could tell, there weren't a lot of other sources for motivation in place at the prison.

"Has anyone heard of TED Talks?" I asked as my class trickled in the next Thursday morning. No one responded, so I explained how TED Talks speakers are among the best speakers in the world and cover just about any imaginable topic. I also told them how attending a presentation in person would cost hundreds of dollars, and possibly thousands, if you were fortunate enough to get a ticket. "We're very lucky that we live in a time where I'm able to bring the best speakers in the world to you in prison at no cost, so I hope you appreciate their messages. We're going to start today's class with one of these TED Talks. It's about regret, something we all have to deal with." I had the DVD ready and started the video. "If everyone pays attention, this lady's going to show us her tattoo."

I was careful not to make eye contact with Jacob, hoping he'd get the message without me bringing any more attention to him or his actions. When the TED Talk finished, I tried to transition to class material.

"We all have regrets." I let that sink in. "In our personal lives and in business, we all make mistakes, and we all have to learn to live with the regret that follows and be thankful we feel it so we can learn from it and move forward as a better person."

"Great message," my TV removal accomplice, Darius, said. "Thank you, man."

One of the many things I learned about teaching in prison was that you don't always know if your message was received or who received it. Although I was hoping Jacob would get something out of that TED Talk, I'd never know. He spent the next three weeks sleeping in class—not just nodding off, but full-blown sleeping with his head down on his desk the whole time, even when we took breaks. I was fairly confident he was on some heavy depressants, although I wasn't sure if they were prison-issued or if he'd gotten them through the prison underground. I ignored the situation because I wasn't sure what else to do about it.

Jacob got out of his chair sleepily one day after class, and on his way out, I naively said, "It must be really hard to get good sleep in here."

Jacob didn't take the bait, though. He gave me a distant "You have no idea" look and was out the door. On the fourth week, though, Jacob was wide-awake and participating.

"Welcome back, Jacob," I told him. "We need your contributions in this class, so it's nice to have you back."

Jacob stopped showing up around week seven, and when I asked the class where he was, I received mostly vague expressions. A student finally spoke up and told me he thought Jacob had been moved to a different prison, but he didn't know why.

As usual, Jack straightened me out after class ended. "You can't ask questions like that," he explained sternly. "To them, that's like snitching on him. In here, everyone's supposed to mind their own business."

Jack had become an ally of sorts by that time. He'd sized me up early and quickly realized I was wildly out of my element in the prison setting. He did his best to show me the ropes, and the first few weeks wouldn't have gone as smoothly without his help. I learned that Jack had left the Marine Corps and taken a job as a salesman at a gutter guard company. He quickly worked his way up to sales manager and quadrupled the company's sales in a little over a year.

As we got into the sales and marketing part, Jack took a big interest. He suggested we set up a mock sales presentation for the rest of the class. Jack acted as the salesman, and I played the prospective customer. I was teaching about negotiation and anchor points, and Jack, who was truly a master at closing the deal, provided a strong sample of the sales process. He started with a proposal of $5,000, and through a somewhat lengthy negotiation, convinced me to agree to a $3,500 gutter replacement for my house. The class seemed to enjoy watching the give-and-take, and it was obvious Jack was enjoying the feelings of normalcy that came with being able to once again practice his craft. When it was over, I asked Jack about the lowest price he would've agreed to.

He gave me a sneery sort of smile and said, "Anything over $2,500 was pure gravy. I always started at twice my cost."

He put together a solid business plan on sales consulting, wanting to call his future business "No Limits." Jack planned to find businesses that were struggling with sales, figure out what they were doing wrong, and fix it—just like he'd done for the gutter replacement franchise.

"I've taken just about every class the North Carolina prison system offers," Jack told me. "When I get out, I'm lining the walls of my office with all the certificates I've earned to show people I used my time in prison wisely."

Jack would sometimes hang around after class and once told me he didn't heed the warnings that would've prevented his prison stay. "The people I worked with told me to slow down, that I was going to self-destruct, but I didn't listen," he explained. Jack started making a lot of money in the gutter guard business and bought a Cadillac SUV that he frequently drove to a bar on his way home. "I was over-tipping them, and they were overserving me," he explained. "I know now that I should've slowed down, but I was working day and night and using alcohol to unwind from it all. It caught up with me, though, that's for sure, and I've got eighteen more months here. But I need this time to honor the life I took."

That was all he said about the matter, but curiosity got the best of me. I once again went against my self-imposed rule and looked Jack up.

Jack was on his way home from that bar in his Cadillac when he hit a young couple driving a moped on a Charlotte city street. As I read about it, I remembered seeing the incident in the newspaper when it happened. The kids had been at a local park sketching flowers that day, and Jack had dragged them for an entire block, probably unaware he'd hit them. The reporter polarized the innocent, young art students on their tiny moped and the thoughtless drunk driver in his big car. The story said, after his sentencing, Jack turned and faced the family and apologized for his actions, telling them that if he could trade places with the victims, he would.

I thought back to the times I'd drive after drinking in my youth with no thoughts of the consequences—how easily it could be me taking Jack's class if things had worked out differently.

Darius sat next to Jack at the table front and center and developed a business plan for a commercial cleaning company. It was no accident that the college combined commercial cleaning with entrepreneurship. The perfect company to start would be a cleaning company, and I always encouraged my students who couldn't come up with a business idea to consider that.

"Everything needs to be cleaned," I'd explain. "You can start a cleaning company with almost no capital, and you don't have to worry about foreign competition. Cleaning services can't be imported."

I wouldn't let those who identified a cleaning company for their business plan get away with just cleaning, though. I always encouraged them to put a twist on the value proposition and try to find something no one else was doing. When we got to the sales and marketing part of the class, we'd practice elevator pitches.

"You've got my attention for about thirty seconds, tops," I told them. "You have to hit me with something interesting."

Darius decided he'd combine his cleaning service with electrician services, which made sense. Once he had the confidence of his customers with cleaning, he could integrate servicing their electrical needs.

Darius talked a lot about a youth football league he had helped start in his hometown. One day, as a reward for his efforts, I surprised Darius with some YouTube footage of his youth team in the playoffs.

Darius watched the video with a faraway look, and afterward, walked over and put his hand on my shoulder. “Thank you, man. That was a nice thing you did for me.”

CHAPTER EIGHT

Trust

"The best way to find out if you can trust somebody is to trust them."

—Ernest Hemingway, American novelist

SOME OF THE GUYS I met in prison warmed up to me right away. Others were slower about it. Some never did. The trust took longer to earn in the first class than in others because I was a complete outsider with no track record. The first man to walk in the door on day one was one of the more physically intimidating guys there. Andre was a stocky but physically fit guy with an icy stare. He had long dreadlocks that he wore in an African-themed Rastafarian cap and initially picked a table close to the front of the room, making sure I could see he was completely disinterested in anything I had to say.

Andre didn't do anything but stare at me for the first two weeks before he loosened up and told me he had once run a business. He would rent restaurant or office space and turn it into a type of bar on weekends. He never got a liquor license, but was able to arrange for pool tables, video games, and entertainment to be brought in. Some family members would promote weekend events on Facebook, and they apparently made decent money at it.

One day, Andre passed me a note that said, "Mr. Moose,

what do I do if I'm running an all-cash business and the police find the money? Can they take it?"

I gave it some thought and found some information for him on the importance of recordkeeping. I'd learned that lesson myself the hard way with my father. At our next break, I sat down with Andre and gave him the best advice I could.

"If you keep records and pay taxes, no one can take your money from you," I told him. "If they catch you walking around with a lot of undeclared cash, they're going to take it, and it'll be difficult—if not impossible—to convince them it's not drug money."

Andre lived in a nearby town that had been settled before the Revolutionary War—not a progressive place by any means—and with his rough exterior, I could form a clear mental image of what would happen if the police caught him with a pocketful of hundred-dollar bills.

"You've got a felony on your record now. My advice would be to play it straight from this point forward."

I discovered many of my students were entrepreneurs at heart, they had run side businesses, but almost none of them formed any type of business structure or ever paid any taxes on the income.

I learned a lot from Andre. Once he decided I had his best interests at heart, he was a good friend who went out of his way to greet me on my way in and out of the prison. He gave me some really good advice after his class graduated.

"They're going to test you, Mr. Moose," he said. "People are going to ask you for things and try you. Don't do anything that's going to cost you your job because we need people like you in here."

Among the many unforeseen challenges I faced was the diversity in both age and education level of the students who signed up for the class. Taking the eleven-week commercial cleaning/entrepreneurship course was a way for inmates to both reduce their sentences and curry favor with the powers that be. It often served as a step toward work release, which was the holy grail of the prison experience. Inmates awarded work release jobs got to leave the camp and work a job like a normal person, making their time go faster and, in many cases, providing them with significant money upon their release.

I didn't know about the perks that came with taking prison classes when I took the job. After I learned what the inmates received in exchange for signing up, I was careful not to delude myself that many guys were there for the content of the class and not the fringe benefits, but that became a big part of the challenge for me. I had them for ninety-nine hours of classroom time and hoped that some of what I had to say might sink in and make a difference. Unfortunately, there wasn't much I could do if a student had no interest in what I was trying to teach them.

I got the first taste of that from Wally, an elderly Black man with a lazy eye. Wally sat by the door and didn't contribute much. He was the last one in the class to pick a business idea, and when I told him he was out of time, he reluctantly chose a furniture reupholstery business, a trade he'd learned in another prison. I did everything in my power to convince Wally he had a highly marketable skill, especially in today's world of mass customization. My wife and I had tried to get a couch reupholstered years before and were unable to find anyone to even price the job despite numerous phone calls and emails.

I was genuinely excited for Wally to get out and start his own business, but every bit of encouragement I provided was met with an instant roadblock. I explained to him that we lived in a Starbucks world. Everybody wanted things tailored for their individual tastes, and that included furniture. I told him of our struggles to find an upholsterer and the beauty of him being able to start small with one customer and build the business over time.

"Where am I going to get the tools?" he asked.

"You've got to find a way," I said. "Work for someone in the business and ask to use the tools on the weekend, or get on the internet and find some quality used tools you can afford with your work release money."

I was new at the job and probably pushed too hard. A few weeks later, Wally reported that he'd changed his business plan to landscaping because "It's a lot easier." I didn't do a good job hiding my disappointment.

Among the students in my first class was Dennis, a wiry white guy with a haughty air. Dennis had an array of tattoos, wore thick prison-issued Clark Kent-type glasses, and had a disdain for authority—made obvious by his arrogant grin and air of superiority. I could almost *see* the chip on his shoulder. Dennis smirked his way through the first few weeks of class until we reached the part of choosing a business to start. He then revealed he'd already established a successful motorcycle repair business before he was incarcerated. Once I got Dennis talking about his business, he came alive. He obviously loved motorcycles and discovered early in his career he had a talent for making them faster. He started with his own bike, then fixed up bikes for his friends.

Dennis explained, "I finally had to tell my friends I couldn't do all the work they wanted for free, and they told me they wanted to pay me for it." He'd started in his garage at home and built the business to a four-bay garage with in-house mechanics who specialized in motorcycles. He eventually incorporated cars in the winter when people stopped riding their motorcycles.

Dennis became a tremendous asset to the class. I downloaded photos of his business and the bikes and cars he worked on from Instagram and put together a presentation that he gave one afternoon. It was powerful for the other students to see how someone they could relate to had started a business from scratch and was successful. Dennis was a natural marketer. When he needed new customers, he'd fix up a car or bike and take it anywhere his target market would notice. When we got to the financing part of the class, he was able to do financial projections and was ready to hit the ground running—with one exception. A former employee stole some property from him when he found out Dennis had been arrested and, more than once, Dennis told me he was going to get even with the guy. I tried to stay out of my students' personal lives, but after hearing Dennis's revenge plan for the second or third time, I advised him to let it go and focus on getting his business restarted instead of the past, or he might end up back in prison, unable to fix any motorcycles for a very long time.

I saw Dennis a few times after his class graduated. He mostly kept to himself and usually had the same arrogant look about him. I never knew what happened, but one day, I realized Dennis was gone from the camp. I saw him again about six months later when he came in and asked for a spare composition notebook so that he could teach someone to play the drums in the prison chapel. Gone was his usual arrogance. He stared at the floor and barely made eye contact. I made an effort to chat when I delivered his book the next week. Grudgingly, he explained he'd been moved from our minimum-security camp to a medium-security camp.

"It was a scary place," Dennis said. "They just warehouse guys there. You might have a serial killer sleeping in the bunk next to you. These guys are never getting out and have nothing to lose. They'd just as soon stab you as shake your hand."

Dennis had that sort of faraway look about him, like he was saying it out of politeness, not that I could possibly understand where he'd been. If the prison system was trying to take

Dennis down a notch, it had succeeded. He'd lost his cocky swagger and seemed ready to put his prison life behind him.

"I've got an eight-year-old daughter," he told me. "I just want to get out of here and try to feel normal again."

Among the many things I discovered during my teaching experience was the interest my students had in money. Because I didn't have enough entrepreneurship material to fill the eleven-week course, I devoted three weeks to principles of personal finance. I began to realize that starting and running a small business was out of the realm of possibility for many of my students, but they all had a relationship with money.

I focused initially on saving. The *Ice House* book fit perfectly in that area, as Uncle Cleve's money principles were straightforward: "You gotta save to have."[2]

For the first few classes, I used the only tool that had been given to me: the copies of Dave Ramsey's book, *Financial Peace*, which taught the importance of working toward debt-free living. I carried the copies over from the programs office and handed them out with the explanation that *these* books had to be returned. I dug deeper into breaking out of the debt cycle and started the topic with statistics to illustrate the fact that more than 50 percent of Americans lived paycheck to paycheck with no savings.

I received a few questions about credit scores—what they were and how to improve them. Although almost everyone checked it online, there was still a process in place where you could mail in the request. For the next class, I brought credit score request forms so anyone could request theirs through the mail. I explained to the class that everyone could request their score once per year at no cost. Although it took several weeks, most of the guys received a report and were pleased with the results. They weren't as bad as they'd expected. I continued that for a few more classes, but the report requests started coming back denied due to "no proof of address," so

I figured whoever handled the mail-in requests was getting tired of seeing a flood of them coming from the same prison.

In future classes, I attempted to illustrate the power of compound interest with an individual retirement account (IRA) that I'd started decades earlier. I put $4,000 into an IRA in the early '90s, placed it in an aggressive mutual fund, and hadn't touched it. I had a contest in each class to see who could come the closest to guessing the current value of the $4,000 twenty-eight years later. It was worth around $65,000 at the time and provided a good real-life example of what could happen when you put a little money away in a tax-free vehicle over a long period of time.

To help explain investing in the stock market, I found a video by an inmate in San Quentin who'd entered prison illiterate and learned to read, write, and eventually trade penny stocks. At the request of a student, I put together a presentation on IRAs, traditional versus Roth, and health savings accounts. I always tried to emphasize that finding a legal way to avoid taxes was the key to getting ahead in investing.

My next financial topic was real estate investing. Many of my students would eventually be released with a sizable sum of money from the work release program, and I thought a down payment on a rental property would be a great place to put it. On YouTube, I found a series of videos made by a former drug dealer who started with one rental property and built a real estate empire worth millions of dollars in assets. He used his videos to help illustrate my concept that real estate doesn't care what color you are or how many felonies you have.

I often moved too fast through the personal finance material for some of the students who had little money literacy, but that was always a challenge of teaching to a diverse group. The material had to make sense to the financial novice and not bore the experienced investor.

Once I got into the financial material, my classes gained some outsiders who'd sit through that part of the class every time I gave it. I asked many times how I could better teach the topic and usually got the answer, "Just keep doing what you're doing, Mr. Moose. It's sinking in."

I made a slideshow from a card game, Habitudes, which used color-coded statement cards, in an attempt to spice up the financial part. Each slide would show a statement like, "If I get some money unexpectedly, I feel like I can spend it any way I want to." The students would either agree or disagree with each statement and mark the appropriate column on a color-coded scoring sheet. At the end of the slide deck, whichever column had the most marks would classify the student into one of six categories: planning, status, giving, saving, security, and carefree. That exercise provided some good discussion material and made the financial material personally relevant for many.

In my later classes, I borrowed a case study from the book *Rich Dad Poor Dad* to illustrate that money should be put into assets. It defined assets as "anything that puts money in your wallet" as opposed to liabilities, which were defined as "anything that takes money out of your wallet." By that definition, even a house purchase would be categorized as a liability unless it was rented to a third party. That was an attempt to illustrate the importance of finding sources of passive income.

With a few weeks remaining, I moved from the money management part of my class to marketing. Coming from a sales background, marketing was my favorite topic. I tried to put together some entertaining presentations showing the importance of determining what the value proposition was for each individual business and evaluating who would be willing to pay for it. I used a presentation on how Subaru targeted lesbian consumers years ago as an example of identifying and catering to your target market. I also covered the power of branding, the fundamentals of personal selling, and cause marketing. Part of the business plan was to connect the business with a charitable cause, which had become incredibly important in today's business environment.

As my first class wound down to the final week, I arranged to have a guest speaker come in for my second-to-last class. The organization that promoted entrepreneurship for ex-offenders agreed to send a former inmate who had become a small business owner for a two-hour presentation. Instead of asking permission from Mr. Clean, I met my guest speaker at the guardhouse in the morning, and we entered the prison together. No one at the guardhouse asked any questions, so I figured it was okay. When we arrived at the dayroom, he gave an inspirational presentation that kept everyone's full attention. He spoke candidly about his time served and how he realized that running his own business was the best way to spend the rest of his life.

I saved the last class for determination. My message was: "The difference between who makes it and who doesn't has little to do with who's smarter or who works harder. The people who make it are the people who refuse to quit."

I found stories of successful people who were one step away from quitting and persevered only because they dug in their heels and found a way to turn things around. Since that was exactly what had happened to me, I could draw from personal experience.

With twenty minutes to go, I played a video on how Sylvester Stallone had been down to his last dollar and refused to sell the script for *Rocky* unless he got the lead role. Stallone vowed to bury his script in the backyard and let the caterpillars play Rocky before he would give up on his dream. It was the best example I knew that illustrated the "never say die" mindset it took for a start-up business to succeed. It was a perfect, fitting way to end the class.

I spent eleven weeks with my first class, and we'd learned a lot from each other. It was obvious I'd been operating without a safety net in an unfamiliar environment, but most of the guys were sympathetic and realized I was only there to try to help them. In my small corner of the prison, it was easy for me to forget my students were anything other than future small business owners.

From day one, I referred to them by their first names like I would anyone else I dealt with in a business setting. Unbeknownst to me, the typical inmate was called by his last name or a nickname by other inmates, and correction officers and other staff members often referred to them by their prison-issued number. I had a few guys correct me or ask me to call them by their nickname or their Islamic name, but most guys seemed to be okay with me using their first name. I decided after a few classes that being called by their first name might make them feel a bit more normal, so I made it a practice in all future classes.

Teaching the first class was even more enjoyable than I expected, and I looked forward to each and every class after that. Richard unexpectedly appeared during one of my last classes, explaining that there would be a graduation ceremony in the chapel after we finished our schedule. I wasn't sure what type of ceremony to expect, but I knew as part of the graduation that each student was supposed to give a presentation to the group on the business plan they'd created. As a result, they'd all receive a very nice certificate from the college signed by yours truly.

Jack, who had played a key role in helping me get oriented in the unfamiliar prison environment, stayed late one day when my first class was finishing up. He asked if he could be an assistant teacher for the next class. I was gung-ho about the idea and told him he could, but he reminded me I'd need permission from the powers that be, so I promised him I'd ask Mr. Clean. As much as I was trying to stay away from Mr. Clean and the programs office, I had three reasons to pay him a visit and grudgingly did so after my first class met for the last time.

The first reason pertained to my wife. I talked about my students at home so much that she'd learned most of their names. She handled collecting the past-due amounts for my company, so I used her as an example of how to use an outside source to assist in the collection process in the cash flow part of my class. Even though she weighed about 110 pounds soaking wet, she was a tiger on the phone. At work, we called her our "Bulldog" because of her collecting ferociousness, and many of my students liked to hear stories about the tactics the Bulldog used to get us paid what we were owed. Since Reba had heard so many stories about the guys I was teaching, I hoped I could bring her to our graduation.

Mr. Clean sat in his usual position, hunched behind the oversized computer monitor, glowering at the screen. I stood outside his office until I realized he wasn't going to invite me in, so I finally entered and sat down sideways in the metal folding chair reserved for visitors.

He reared his head long enough to briefly make eye contact and shoot me an inquisitive look.

"This graduation ceremony—is that something someone might bring their wife to?" I asked innocently.

Mr. Clean gave it no consideration at all. "It's not" was his instant reply.

"Okay." I continued. "A student has expressed interest in being an assistant instructor for the next class. Is that something we could arrange?"

Mr. Clean asked who it was, so I gave him Jack's name, and he began typing on his keyboard. "That's not going to happen." Mr. Clean glanced at me with a pained look and added, "Is there anything else?"

I'd planned to ask when I could expect my key to the programs office, as had been promised, but figured my best plan of action was to make a quick exit because all my requests were getting shot down so quickly. I also decided I wasn't going to ask Mr. Clean for permission anymore if I could help it.

Despite being denied an invitation to my first class's graduation ceremony, my wife graciously baked several batches of brownies for the guys, which proved to be popular—especially with Sampson. Our first graduation was on the Wednesday after I'd finished our final class meeting and started at 8:00 a.m., the same time the class started. I looked forward to spending time with my students in a fun environment and showing them some appreciation for the effort they'd put in.

CHAPTER NINE
Back to Reality

"There are no facts, only interpretations."
—Friedrich Nietzsche, German philosopher

MY HIGH EXPECTATIONS FOR THE graduation ceremony were quickly deflated, and the experience soon made clear the reality of what it was like to be incarcerated. In the isolated dayroom, I could treat the guys how I wanted to treat them, call them by their first names, and consider them to be future small business owners. The graduation of the first class was the first time I witnessed how my students were treated by everyone else in the prison—a real eye-opener. The men I'd come to know over the past eleven weeks were treated as objects, not people, by the prison officials. They were told to "line up" and "shut up" and were threatened with loss of privileges for any sort of misbehavior. One student had been found with tobacco in his locker and was told he couldn't participate in the ceremony, then told he could, then again told he couldn't. It seemed those in charge were enjoying the control they had over the inmates who'd taken the class. They were students to me, but just faceless numbers to a majority of the prison staff.

I brought a camera to that first graduation ceremony, not realizing it was against the rules. I'd wanted to take pictures with my students so that my wife could connect some names to faces.

"Don't let them see that camera," Richard warned me after watching me taking a few snapshots. "They won't like it."

The graduation started with the student presentations on their business plans. I spent some class time during the final week on public speaking and offered the opportunity to practice in front of the class. Some were natural presenters and explained business plans in detail—both concepts and execution. Others were terrified to get up in front of the group. Even though they were presenting to me, Richard, and fellow students they'd spent the last eleven weeks with, the natural fear of talking in front of a group was an obstacle difficult for many to overcome in all of my classes. I tried to challenge any student who appeared uncomfortable to get up, get it over with, and learn from the experience, but I was also quick to give a pass to anyone who looked truly terrified.

During their presentations, many students made it a point to thank me and Richard for our efforts, and I extended an invitation to the graduates to return to my next class and help the new students whenever they could. That was met with a quizzical look from Richard, who was also wondering who the heck Sampson was and why he was giving a presentation on his wine business when he wasn't registered for the class.

"Don't let the college find out about this," he warned after I explained my open-door policy. "They won't like it."

After the presentations, Richard and I made a salad in the small chapel kitchen while the graduates watched *The Avengers* on the big movie screen in the meeting area. Richard and I left the camp to pick up pizza and chicken, and our graduates enjoyed a huge lunch with food that many said they hadn't eaten in years. Richard baked a pound cake for dessert, mixing nicely with my wife's brownies. It was a long day. I left the prison around 2:00 p.m. and had Richard open the back gate for me since I still didn't have a key.

I drove home with mixed emotions. I was grateful for the opportunity to try to help some of the guys I'd met in prison change the course of their lives, but I also realized my efforts were going to be severely hindered by the prison infrastructure. Despite my efforts to get my students thinking like small business owners, they were in an environment that, by design, dehumanized them. It was like running a footrace while dragging an anchor behind me. In planning for my second class, I hoped to be left alone in my little classroom two mornings a week and provided with the freedom to put together a class that would best serve my students.

* * *

I had a week off from teaching before the start of my second class, which was scheduled to start in mid-July. It gave me extra time to prepare, although I was much more confident the second time around. I'd learned a tremendous amount from the first class and started a working outline for the course—considerably more than I had to work with when I started. I was gradually beginning to feel like a teacher.

With my newfound swagger, I decided to start the class a little differently by giving an assignment on the first day to complete before we met again a day later. That would get the students involved in the material early and show I expected them to put in some work in order to get their entrepreneurship certificate.

Shortly after graduation, Richard emailed me the next class roster. It had the mugshots and names of the ten men who'd signed up. The last column read "Items of Note." There was a notation in that column for one of the guys, Pete, that read: "Escapes: Y." It seemed that Pete had made a dash for the gate at some point in his prison career, and I wasn't sure what I was supposed to do if I saw him climbing the fence.

I needn't have worried. Pete turned out to be a fifty-year-old white guy whose scars and weariness represented someone who'd had a tough fifty years. His tired and timid demeanor was not what I expected from a former prison escapee.

The tiny wall-mounted air conditioner in G Dorm worked overtime to keep us cool in the July morning of the first day of class. Shortly after the count cleared, my new students began to drift into the dayroom. The racial makeup differed this time. Instead of the four-to-one Black-to-white ratio of my first class, I had an even mix: five white guys and five Black guys.

I introduced myself, then went around the room asking for names, business experience, and ideas for a type of business they'd like to run. Former escapee Pete had selected a table in the back of the room and, when called on, explained he'd worked in the family flooring business his whole life and even had a stint running his own flooring business. He was exactly the type of student I needed, someone who could help me illustrate small business principles with their real-life experience. When I challenged the class to give fifty reasons to start their own businesses, Pete came up with at least half of them and was quick to illustrate the good parts of being your own boss.

As our class time neared the end, I handed each student a copy of *Ice House* and instructed them to read chapter one and complete six discussion questions I'd created. The first chapter of *Who Owns the Ice House?* was the longest of the book—twenty-four pages—so I expected the assignment to be challenging for some of the guys, especially since they had less than twenty-four hours to complete it and answer the discussion questions.

From my undergraduate days, I remembered certain

professors who loaded students with lengthy assignments on the first day. They did it to send a message that the class wouldn't be easy and would require considerable effort. I felt confident that utilizing that strategy would result in more serious students and a better class. Although reading one chapter of a book and answering six questions wasn't an overly taxing task, I was proud of myself for using a tried-and-true educational strategy and was eager to see the results.

Then, the next class began.

My well-thought-out plan completely blew up in my face. I arrived Friday morning and found a distraught Pete pacing the floor of the dayroom. He had the room to himself since they hadn't cleared count yet. Pete stopped pacing and got right to the point as soon as I entered the dorm.

"I can't do this, man," he said. "I've got a meth problem. My brain don't work right anymore." He continued to pace the floor as he resumed his rant. "I read the chapter, but I can't remember any of it, so I kept having to go back and reread it to answer those questions you gave us, and I was up all night." With an exhausted look, Pete handed me the half-filled discussion question sheet with frantic-looking scribbles. He stood toe-to-toe with me, looking very determined. "I want out. I done told them that in programs this morning."

I spent the next ten minutes trying to calm Pete down, explaining that the assignment wasn't going to matter. The class was pass/fail, and everyone who attended the class passed.

"I need you in this class," I told him. "You can help these guys learn the material with your business experience."

Pete would have none of it, though. "I'm sorry, man. I've got to get out of this class." He'd made up his mind, and there was nothing I could do to bring him back.

I thought it was my duty to let the head of programs know Pete wanted out of my class, so I emailed Mr. Clean when I got back to Charlotte and explained the situation, asking him to let me keep Pete in class now that I was aware of his limitations.

I never got an email back from Mr. Clean, and I never saw Pete again. That was another of my many rookie mistakes. I was getting guys from all different education levels, some with college degrees, and some who could barely write. It was impossible to provide an assignment that would work for the whole group. The majority of my class material was too simple for the educated students and too challenging for the ones with limited formal education. I learned from Pete that it was best to cover the material in class and not assign anything except simple reading. After that experience, I eased my students into all future homework and kept my expectations low.

Even though we lost a student on the second day, that class had a chemistry I was never able to duplicate. It was the right mix of people at the right time.

My star student was a lanky guy named Raymond. He was about my age and a light-skinned African American who kept his hair neatly trimmed and had a welcoming smile. Raymond had a certain discipline about him; he kept his clothes clean and often scolded the other students who weren't taking my class seriously. He sat front and center at the same table as Jack and Darius. I was starting to see a pattern: the guys who were there to learn sat there. Raymond had spent some time in the military, and as the class progressed, I learned three other students in that class had a military background, which might have contributed to the self-discipline and respect they extended to me.

When it was Raymond's turn to discuss the business he wanted to start, he didn't hesitate. "I'm not supposed to be in this camp. I was put here by mistake," he began. "But when I got here, they signed me up for the cleaning class, which I didn't want to take. Then, I found out about this business part, and I've been thinking of a business plan for a while, so maybe all this happened for a reason." Raymond had my full attention. "The name of my company is going to be MOTH, which stands for 'Men of the Harvest.' The name is in reference to the Bible verse, Matthew 9:37, where Jesus says the harvest is plentiful, but the laborers are few. I'm going to start a nonprofit corporation that helps formerly incarcerated men find jobs. I can be a spokesperson for these guys and also act as a go-between for the employer and the employees. There are some talented men in places like this, but some need an agent to vouch for them in order to get their chance once they get out. I can be that agent."

At that point, most students didn't have an idea for a business they wanted to start. If they did, they'd typically give me a one-word answer like "painting."

After listening to Raymond's comprehensive business plan, all I could do was stand at my table, slightly bewildered, and think, *Maybe this did all happen for a reason.*

I did a lot of research for his business plan over the next eleven weeks, and we both learned a lot, including how to set up nonprofit companies and how to apply for grants. A student in the class designed a great "Men of the Harvest" logo, a wheat spike around the silhouette of a laborer. Months after our class finished, Raymond was chosen as the first inmate to begin a work release assignment for a nearby textile mill. I told him the prison was sending its best man to start the work release process and that it was similar to the business he wanted to start. Raymond quickly rose to shift leader at the mill and, according to some mutual friends, got married shortly after his release.

A positive influence in the class was a young, jovial Black man, Marcus, who wanted to open a barber shop. Marcus's good-natured spirit was rare in the prison environment. He always smiled, laughed, and agreed with whatever was said in class. One day after break, a couple of students asked me to count the number of fingers on Marcus's hand as Marcus held it out. I counted six, counted again, and got six. I looked quizzically at them, waiting for them to reveal their trick, but there was no magic to it.

"I've got six toes on each foot too," Marcus explained. About halfway through the class, Marcus moved to the table with the view of the garden, which by that time, was full of ripening squash, cucumbers, watermelons, corn, and okra. Marcus was still his same overly friendly self, but he was mentally miles away. Following his unseeing gaze, I looked out at the view of the garden. I recognized the middle-aged burly man with a full beard who seemed to always be out in the field working. I'd seen the guy in passing before. Wearing his prison-issued green and gray, he would sometimes drive an old tractor down Palisade Prison Road between the gravel lot and the garden. I figured he must be some sort of trustee because he seemed to be free to go wherever he wanted, even outside the prison fence.

An elderly inmate, Alan, was also in my second class. At first, it seemed Alan had made up his mind that there was no changing his future.

"I went to see my daddy in prison, and now my son's in prison, too. Ain't that something?" he told me one day for no particular reason.

"It's up to you to break the cycle," I challenged him, which was met with a polite smile and a look that told me he had no plans to do anything like that.

When I got into the real estate part of my course, something about Alan changed. He started to pay close attention, ask questions, and one day, brought a note to me after class.

"My family has some land in South Carolina," it read. "Do you think you could get some prices on what a mobile home might cost? I'm thinking about putting one on that land and renting it out."

From that point forward, Alan was a more focused man. He told me that when class started, he couldn't make himself read the *Ice House* book, but now he couldn't put it down.

When our last class ended, Alan was the last to leave. He stayed in the dayroom looking around, then lingered in the doorway while telling me all his real estate plans, like he didn't want the class to end. In my tenure as a prison teacher, Alan was one of the first guys I felt had received my message. It was as if I'd helped him realize for the first time that he was in control of his future and didn't have to spend the rest of his life going in and out of prisons if he didn't want to.

At the center table of the classroom sat a short, solemn, middle-aged man named Victor. He was from Queens, New York, and had the accent and mannerisms of a streetwise New Yorker. I learned halfway through the class that Victor had a wife and young twin sons at home who relied on social services and the generosity of family to survive. He had some business experience consisting of selling stereo equipment at his small retail store, a car detailing service, and a variety of other small businesses over the years. While Victor had good business sense, he'd never kept records or paid taxes. He'd sometimes have a lot to say but, at other times, would be silent for weeks at a time.

His business plan was to be a motivational speaker. He wanted to help kids who were starting down the road he'd gone down—the wrong road, but one spurred by his horrific past—to choose a different path. Victor had appalling stories of the foster homes he and his brother lived in, with heroin-addicted caretakers who had, more than once, held them by their heels out the window of a high-rise in Queens.

Upon learning of his plans to become a motivational speaker, I challenged Victor to join the international speaking club, Toastmasters, after his release to get in the practice of public speaking.

"You ever been?" Victor wanted to know.

I told him I'd gone to a meeting once, but thought the format was a little stale.

"What do you mean by that?" he asked.

I told him that before the meeting, we all faced the flag and said the Pledge of Allegiance, which seemed out of place to me and dated. "I haven't said the Pledge of Allegiance since the Boy Scouts," I explained.

The thought of me saying the Pledge of Allegiance against my will set Victor into a fit of hysterics. He was laughing so hard he nearly fell out of his chair.

"They made him say the Pledge of Allegiance," Victor sputtered between bursts of laughter, pointing at me the whole time. His laughter got me laughing about the absurdity of the situation, and we shared a rare moment of levity while the rest of the class gawked. From that day on, every time Victor entered the classroom or when we saw each other in the yard, we'd try to be the first one to cover our hearts with our right hands and point at each other—our little inside joke.

By the third week of the class, each student was supposed to have a business idea, a name for their start-up, and an idea for some sort of logo. The name of Victor's motivational speaker business was "A Boy Becomes a Man." It took us weeks to come up with a logo he liked. It showed a young African American boy on the streets of New York carrying his possessions in a black plastic garbage bag. I added "When a Man Is Needed" to complete the quote.

His experience as a motivational speaker consisted of one presentation that he'd given impromptu to a junior high student body years before. Throughout our eleven weeks of class, I encouraged Victor to practice by giving the class a motivational speech, to which he always responded, "You don't understand, man" or "I can't do that here."

Victor saved his speech for graduation, where he got up

and explained to the class that the choices that landed them in prison were having a terrible impact on the people they cared most about. Leaning over our makeshift podium, Victor reprimanded the class for making choices that put them in their current position where they couldn't take care of their families.

"Every time we call home and ask for money to be put in our commissary accounts, we're taking food out of the mouths of our children," he preached. As Victor continued his speech, what started as a challenge to the class gradually became an admission of his failure. At the end, Victor stood there speechless and unable to continue, tears flowing down his face. Realizing Victor had become too emotional to complete his homily, a student rose, handed Victor some paper towels to dry his tears, and gave him a hug.

I finally understood what Victor had been trying to tell me. He didn't need practice. When he spoke, he spoke completely from the heart. We were all stunned at the outpour of his heartfelt emotions, which were rarely seen in the stoic prison environment, and it added to the bond the class had as a group and made for a memorable graduation.

My serial entrepreneur, Sampson, who hadn't missed a class since my first day, was so inspired by Victor's emotional outburst he wrote a short poem titled "Situations" and delivered it impromptu to the group.

Raymond talked about how much he loved God and how thankful he was for my class, which had given him an unexpected, positive direction in his life. I was blown away by how transparent and trusting we'd grown with each other. Richard silently watched the proceedings from the back of the room and shot me a puzzled look. That ceremony wasn't what anyone had expected, but it was one of my greatest days as a teacher. I felt like I'd somehow facilitated the chemistry of the group and provided them with some hope for their futures. It was a powerful morning, and I didn't want it to end. I knew we'd never all be together as a group again, and the special bond we'd created would be difficult, if not impossible, to duplicate with any other class.

My second class was the first one I surveyed. I asked my students to complete a ten-question survey—with instructions to be as honest as possible.

"Don't worry about saying anything negative about me or my class," I told them. "I can take it, and it'll only make the next class better."

I was hoping to get some insight into what I could do better, but the surveys all came back with positive comments. Among the feedback was what Victor provided when asked how the class had changed his thinking: "I know now that I am not a loser."

CHAPTER TEN

Adjusting to the New Normal

"Treat people as if they were what they ought to be and you help them to become what they are capable of being."

—Johann Wolfgang von Goethe, German novelist

I USUALLY GOT A WEEK off between graduation and the start of each new class, which was greatly appreciated and sorely needed. Besides the long weekends typing business plans and the two half-days teaching—plus the drive there and back—I was still working forty-plus hour weeks at my locker company. Any time off was a blessing. I dedicated the extra time to preparing for the next class. Although I still fell short on material, I didn't worry as much about running out of things to talk about. My two classes had given me much-needed confidence, and because I started fresh every eleven weeks, the material was slightly more polished every time I used it.

I returned to the prison to start my third class in the middle of October. The crops in the garden had been harvested, and the bearded man was hard at work cleaning things up and getting his soil ready for the next spring. The class would run through the Thanksgiving and Christmas holidays and was scheduled to graduate in mid-January.

Something had changed in regard to the trust level I felt from both the students and even prison staff by that point. It took many weeks in my first class and a few classes in my second class to earn the trust of my students. That seemed to change. Apparently, the word was out that Mr. Moose was okay and there to help. I'd become known as the guy who could get you something—a notebook, a pen, a book, or some information on a business you wanted to start—and asked for nothing in return except that you give his class an honest effort.

The guards who had thoroughly searched my bags at first mostly waved me through, with the exception of the old guy who had given me trouble the first few weeks. He still searched my things from time to time, but it was getting to be routine for him. Because he wasn't finding any contraband, I could tell his heart really wasn't in it anymore.

I'd been teaching for six months, and my new challenge became the delays I'd face walking across the prison yard before and after class by inmates who wanted to stop and talk. Former and current students hindered my progress, along with others who wanted to introduce themselves. Sometimes the seventy-yard walk would take as long as twenty minutes. At first, I found that to be inconvenient, but as I got to know the guys, I enjoyed stopping and talking. I was always met with respect, smiles, handshakes, questions about a potential business idea, or them wanting to know how my wife, the Bulldog, was doing. I realized I was probably a rare taste of the outside world to them, someone who would call them by their first name, shake their hand, and look them in the eye.

My early instructions were to only temporarily give out materials and collect everything at the end of class. By my third class, I decided to do what I thought was necessary to make the course better and give the students who wanted to improve themselves the materials they needed to have a fighting chance once they got released. It was nearly impossible for me to say no to anyone who requested a book, but I was careful not to overtly break the rules. Books and other handouts had to be business related.

In attempts to wake up my students, I'd sometimes have content-related contests and provide the winner with any book that was available on Amazon. A young inmate had the closest guess to "What percentage of millionaires became so due to real estate investing?" and won one of my book contests early in my teaching career. He wanted a tattoo magazine to get ideas for his future tattoo business. The magazine looked pretty racy when it arrived, but a guard confirmed it was okay to bring in.

Once the guys learned I was a source for educational materials, I was buying notebooks and pens in bulk and had enough *Ice House* and other business and motivational books circulating the prison that they could've stocked a small library. Maybe it was all the free items, but my class slowly gained popularity. The head of programs told me when I first started that he had to transfer guys in from other prisons to fill the roster, but I learned there was a waiting list of those already housed in the prison wanting to sign up.

The students who comprised my third class were hardworking and respectful, and I formed relationships that lasted the rest of my time at the prison. A good indicator of how each class would run came toward the end of the first meeting when I'd ask for businesses anyone would like to start or for businesses they'd worked for previously. It was always a huge plus to have someone who'd started one—they could illustrate the class principles with their experiences.

It was about that time Anthony Williams began showing up. He was an elderly Black man with a distinguished disposition. He'd sit at the table by the door and, like many others, seemed to get a kick out of my class. Anthony was from New

York and once brought in pictures of himself with some celebrities, dressed to the nines in every photograph.

"Because I dressed nice and drove a nice car, a lot of people thought I was a drug dealer," Anthony explained. "In fact, I'm in here for a drug charge, but I've never sold drugs in my life."

Anthony wrote a book about the circumstances leading up to his arrest and undeserved prison sentence and started asking me to buy a copy from the first day I met him. I finally gave in, bought his book, and had him sign it. I enjoyed reading it. He was a gifted writer and told his story well.

One day, Anthony asked if I wanted to promote his next project, a website that would publish stories and poems written by prison inmates who were incarcerated. I turned down his offer, but was impressed with his drive and business sense. He'd been locked up for years but wasn't letting it stop him from what he wanted to accomplish.

The third class also had Levi Parker, a young African American who explained to me that he had once operated a handyman business.

"No job too small," Levi often said with a toothy ear-to-ear smile that would light up his corner of G Dorm. "I had a good business for a while," he explained. "But I was young and didn't appreciate it."

The "No Job Too Small" motto was exactly how I'd built my locker business. As taught by my father, lots of small orders typically provided a higher profit margin without killing cash flow and tying up resources.

I hoped Levi would be a big help to my teaching efforts, even though he mostly kept to himself. His small business experience put him way ahead of most students. His contributions were always solid, and he built a great handyman business plan. Levi's life goal was to someday drive a red Audi. I encouraged him to pursue that goal but warned him against letting his customers see him driving it.

"If I saw you driving a red Audi around town, I'd think you charged too much for your services," I told him.

My warnings were always met with a huge smile and, "Right on, Mr. Moose. I'll only drive it on Sundays." Or something to that effect.

Levi could be downright charming, and shortly after our class ended, he somehow charmed his way into a third-shift work release job way ahead of the other students. The third-shift work release inmates often got to the prison the same time I did, around 7:45 a.m. As I set up for class, they were eating a quick breakfast and hitting their bunks in G Dorm to try to get some rest before their next late shift. One thing I could count on every morning was that at some point during my class, Levi would appear from behind the rickety partition, swagger up to me, and shake my hand with a friendly "How you doing, Moosey?" while flashing that million-dollar smile. He was one of the guys there who went out of his way to greet me every day.

After my first two classes, I realized that while some students took the business plan part of the course seriously, owning a business was out of reach for a lot of inmates. They'd work on coming up with a good name for their business and a nice logo, but would quit turning in an actual business plan early on.

In my third class, I had such a student, Dominick, a young and portly Black man with a gold front tooth and a huge smile. He wanted to open a night club. "Mack Alley" was the name he finally came up with. Dominick had a vision of a huge club with live music, fully stocked bars, and beautiful ladies all around. It was still early in my teaching, so I'd occasionally ask Dominick what he thought it would cost to open such a place.

"I don't know, Mr. Moose, but I hope you can come see me once I get it up and running," Dominick would say, flashing his gold grill at me. I'd never met a friendlier, more positive guy, and he was so convinced that he'd someday own his bar that I didn't have the heart to dampen his excitement by discussing start-up costs. Dominick spent most of the time working on his logo and skipped over almost all of the parts relating to business fundamentals. I thought it would be totally fitting if Dominick would be the one guy who made it big.

"You know I'll be there, Dominick," I told him. "Can't wait to see it."

A young, somber-looking guy sat in the back of the room and mostly kept quiet. When it was time to share his business idea, he introduced himself as Wayne and explained that he wanted to start a sporting dog registry. Wayne knew the people who ran the only national dog registry that was well-regarded among the sporting dog community and saw a big opportunity to establish himself as a competitor. I learned a lot about the dog registry business thanks to Wayne, and I thought he'd found a great niche in an underserved market.

Wayne put together a well-thought-out business plan and then quickly moved on to a high-paying work release job as a welder after graduation. He would occasionally stop by G Dorm to see me after class and one day told me he'd been offered a position with the company he was working for after his release. "It's probably my best move now that I have a felony," he explained.

"Don't give up on your dog registry idea," I urged him. "It's something you can start while you're working for someone else until it can support you."

Wayne was quick to agree, but added, "Welding is a good opportunity for me, too." It was hard for me to accept that someone with his potential and a great business idea might work for someone else for the rest of his life. Wayne's good behavior while in the prison system had earned him the brass ring of a work release job, and it was easy to understand how that could seem like the brightest possible future to him.

The man who sat front and center for my third class was Benny, a tall, lanky African American with long dreadlocks and a tight smile. Benny was in his late thirties and wanted to be a DJ. He explained that even though he was a lot older than most DJs, the kids got a kick out of him when he performed because of the way he danced. He came in wanting to write three business plans, focusing mostly on one for a cleaning company, which would allow him to raise enough capital to follow his true passion.

I found out Benny was down to a few months until his release date and that his birthday was going to fall on one of our class meetings, so I designed a birthday card with Benny the Ball from the Top Cat cartoon on it and gave it to him with a book on tips for starting a cleaning company.

The next day, Benny handed me a note after class that read, "Yesterday was my thirty-seventh birthday, and all I got was the card and book you gave me. Thank you for doing that, and if you're looking for a friend, I can be a great friend."

Because Benny was down to some short time, I'd try to guess the number of days I thought he had left on his sentence. Every man in there knew exactly how much time he had left, but for Benny, the fast-approaching date didn't elicit the excitement I'd seen in other inmates. Benny came to see me in my classroom the day before he was set to be released. I had a video playing, so I went to the back of the room and sat with him.

"Tomorrow's the big day, right?" I asked.

Benny had his head down but looked up and said, "I've got nothing when I get out: no job, no car, no place to stay. Being in here is easy. I can do this. Living on the outside is what's hard. I've got a few hundred dollars from my work release job, but that's not going to last long. I don't know how I'm going to make it."

I wanted to help Benny. The ex-offender/inmate program that provided my guest speakers was soon expanding to Charlotte, and I'd volunteered to be an instructor for them, as well as let them use my warehouse/office for the weekly meetings. I looked forward to being able to work with potential small business owners without all the restrictions I'd been facing in the prison environment. I encouraged Benny to sign up for the class and attend the meetings, and he agreed to do it.

Benny was true to his word and came to the meetings. It was an eight-week program that met after business hours once a week. It was my first opportunity to spend time with a former student outside of the prison and also the first time I realized my limitations toward providing any tangible help to them in the real world. I had ten new students every eleven weeks, and keeping up with the class work and running my locker business were consuming all my free time and resources. I felt like I'd planted a seed with Benny, possibly inspired him to consider starting his own business, given him eleven weeks' worth of advice and sound business start-up principles, then disappeared at the time he needed me most.

The ex-offender program turned out to be a disappointment for both of us. Although I enjoyed the opportunity to teach, their material was similar to what I used in my class. Instructing inside the prison fence forced me to comply with all the limitations of that environment. The lack of computer software and limited access to outside resources often made me feel like I was swimming upstream. It disappointed me to discover the ex-offender/entrepreneur organization also focused on lectures and didn't take advantage of all the hands-on opportunities readily available in the outside world to help a start-up business. What Benny needed most was someone to show him how to get customers for his cleaning business by making cold calls with him at local business parks, just like Myron did with me decades earlier.

After the second meeting in my warehouse, I met with one of the higher-ups and asked if lecturing was what we were going to be doing for the whole eight-week program.

"I can teach principles in prison," I told him. "These guys are out. They need real-world help now. We should be designing and printing their business cards and making sales calls with them. We can talk all day, but until you go out and get your first customer, you don't have a business."

The local program head candidly told me they realized most of the students were never going to run a business, so the organization instead focused on making them better employees by helping them understand what it was like to start one.

Upon learning that, I thanked Benny for being such a good friend and for attending the meetings, which I knew were an inconvenience for him, but I was okay if he didn't come anymore. Benny was in complete agreement.

He gave me his typical crooked smile and said, "You didn't know it was going to be like this, Mr. Moose. Thank you for trying." He gave me a hug and headed out. He never came back to any of the meetings, and that was the last time I saw him. It was also my last stint as a volunteer with that organization.

* * *

As I walked through the prison yard on a cool November afternoon after a day of teaching, I saw a student from my second class, Marcus, working outside with the portly, bearded man from the garden. They were doing some sort of landscaping inside the prison fence, and I stopped to say hello to Marcus, who was his usual agreeable and overly friendly self. During our discussion, the older man paid me no attention, but I got the impression he was inconspicuously observing how I treated Marcus. Marcus was the type who would generally agree with whatever you said and had a gift of making you feel like the most important person in the room. After deciding I was being respectful and not taking advantage of Marcus's good nature, the bearded man introduced himself as Kendal. Kendal had a thick country accent and once he started talking, he didn't stop for at least ten minutes.

As he began explaining all the planting he'd done and telling me the names of all the flora and fauna encompassing the prison, I slowly realized he was the man who maintained the grounds. I'd seen him working in the gardens many times, but until that day, I didn't realize he was also the mastermind behind the amazing floral displays that turned the prison yard into a botanical garden. He gave me a tour of the camp and pointed out all the beautiful flowering plants, explaining why he put each one where he had and detailing what each plant needed to thrive. It didn't take long to realize Kendal had a gift for all things that grew and an incredible work ethic. I also learned he was responsible for converting the old baseball field into the two-acre farm everyone at camp called "the garden," which was the area Marcus had been staring at during classes.

As I had an interest in growing vegetables, I knew I could learn a lot from Kendal. "Next time you're here, you come down and see me in the garden, and I'll show you around," he promised.

* * *

I was comfortable with my material when my fourth class started, and I decided to start it in a different way. My sales background made me a firm believer in the importance of making a good first impression. For each of my classes, I hoped to find a way to get the students out of their comfort zones and challenge them to pay attention for the next eleven weeks. In order to accomplish that, I put together a presentation showing the incarceration rates for Black people versus white people. The odds of a white person in his thirties being incarcerated is one in eleven. For a Black man, it's one in three.[3]

Then, I showed incarceration rates for the poor versus the rich, equally skewed to favor the wealthy. The third part showed the incarceration rates for the uneducated versus the educated. Fewer than 1 percent of people in prison had a master's degree.

"Why is that?" I challenged them after showing the education disparity. "Can anyone think of a reason why a person with a formal education is less likely to spend time in prison?"

I usually gave up fairly quickly when I failed to get a response from a class, but that time, I let the silence get uncomfortable enough that a young Black man at a middle table finally gave me the one-word response I was looking for.

"Choices," he said with his eyes fixated downward on his table.

"Thank you, that's it exactly!" I urged him to continue, but he stayed quiet. "Typically, the higher our level of education, the more options we have to make money, which makes breaking the law for this reason less attractive. So, unless you're rich, white, and well-educated, my advice to you is to not break the law, because the odds are heavily stacked against you to get any sort of fair deal by the current justice system."

There were no arguments from any of my new students, but I secretly wondered if anyone who might have been watching me on one of those tiny TVs over in the sergeant's office was heading down the narrow sidewalk toward G Dorm to shut down my class.

The second part of my presentation focused on work release. "What's the best thing that could happen to you while you're here in prison?" I asked the class.

That was met with blank stares as if they couldn't imagine anything good happening.

"Work release," I finally answered my own question. "I always hear guys complaining that they don't have it yet. Probably, some of you took this class, hoping it would move you up the list for a work release assignment. That's fine, but please don't let the job you get for work release be the end-all of your working career because I'm here to show you another way."

The class seemed to be paying attention. A couple of guys in the back had sort of an incredulous look, like they couldn't believe what I was saying.

"The money you can make with your hands is limited, but there's no limit to the money you can make with your mind," I continued. "My job here is to encourage you to start your own business when you're released because getting a job with a felony won't be easy, and getting a good job will be even harder."

The best work release job I'd heard of at the prison paid twelve dollars an hour, so I showed a slide I created, outlining the challenges of surviving solo—much less raising a family—on that pay.

Next, I showed the failure rate of small businesses, which varied according to the source, but was always high: less than half of small business start-ups made it through the first year.

"So, you might be thinking, 'Why is this crazy old guy trying to get me to do something that statistically, I'm likely to fail at?'"

My next slide listed the top reasons start-up businesses fail. The list included lack of planning, poor pricing strategy, bad recordkeeping, flawed concept, and being outworked by the competition.

One by one, I eliminated items from the list. "We've got eleven weeks to plan. I'm going to try to help you come up with a break-even point for your business. I'll walk you through the necessary records you have to keep and the taxes you're required to file. When you decide what business you want to start and where you want to start it, I'll get information on your competition, and we'll try to figure out something you can do better than them. There's a chance we won't know if your concept is flawed until you put it into action, but the beauty of being a start-up is that you can change direction quickly until you find something that *does* work."

I couldn't tell if I was encouraging anyone, but they seemed attentive, so I continued. "The only thing I can't help you with is the last one. If you're not willing to work day and night on your start-up business, then I'd encourage you to work for someone else. It won't be easy to take nothing and make it into something, but if you're willing to work harder than you've ever worked in your life and not quit until you make it happen, it can be the most rewarding thing you'll ever do."

I thought my new introduction might serve as a wake-up call and motivate some guys to give my class an honest effort, but I wasn't sure if it succeeded or changed anyone's way of thinking. My students kept their emotions in check, as I was sure they'd been conditioned to do in the prison environment. It was difficult to gauge reactions from a dorm room full of stone-faced people, but it was a fun way to get the new class started, and I used it for every class from that day forward.

In later classes, I added a final word: "I may not be the best instructor in this field, but I'll work as hard as you do on your business plan, and I'm one of the few resources this prison provides for you. If I were you, I'd take full advantage of the opportunity this class presents. In fact, if you can find something better to do at this prison than come to my class, that's fine with me. I'm not going to take attendance, and you'll get a certificate with your name on it like everyone else either way. If you don't want to be here, I'd rather someone who wants to be here take your place."

I thought that last part would be my way of throwing down the gauntlet and might help my students realize my class was an opportunity for them. But instead of accepting the challenge, too many guys took it as a free pass to cut class. If I could do it over again, I would leave my no-attendance-policy challenge out of the opening presentation. It was largely my ego, but I loved challenging my students to come to class only if they wanted to learn so much that I couldn't stop myself from doing it, even when I knew it was being abused. Though I was still learning how to be an effective instructor, my fourth class turned out to mostly be a good group of guys who had some great ideas on start-up businesses and put forth a good effort to create some solid business plans.

I found a book, *The Reverse Effect*, by Clinton McCoy, a former inmate turned entrepreneur. In his book, Clinton outlines a seven-step process for "breaking the chains of the past and unlocking the doors of the future."[4] I contacted him and asked for a bulk rate for his book; I explained that I'd be using them in a prison setting for an entrepreneurship class.

He was cordial and accommodating, and when I asked if he'd sell me fifty books for twelve dollars each, his counteroffer surprised me. "I'll go ten dollars each, but the guys get to keep the books."

The Reverse Effect became a big hit with my students, and I continued to buy them in lots of fifty and show Clinton's YouTube videos in my class.

It was during this class that I realized I was focusing most of my efforts on the students who were putting forth the greatest effort and letting the stragglers slide. I expected every student to complete a business plan, but in my past three classes, I had three or four that either didn't bother to start or would quit the plan at some point during the course. Even with my limited experience, it wasn't hard to tell who the nonparticipators were likely to be on day one.

For the fourth class, I did something different. When our second session began on Friday, I brought in a copy of *The Reverse Effect* for the guys I thought would be the most likely to lose interest. I asked if they'd do me a favor: read the book and let me know if they thought it would be good material for the rest of the students. Taking an interest in those students early paid dividends as they seemed to take interest in class material and would usually report back to me a few weeks later, providing their opinion of the book.

The first guy to speak up in the class was a forty-year-old Will Ferrell look-alike named Henry. He took the front-and-center table and was quick with a smile and a story. I liked him right away. As a way of introducing himself, he told me he'd managed a bar in a coastal resort town in North Carolina for a year and made a lot of money.

"Then I got into cocaine and decided to let the business run itself," he explained. "I learned you can't do that."

Once Henry learned I could bring him things from the outside, he had lots of requests. Some I didn't mind, like a training chart for a bench press lifting plan, but some I did, like weight-lifting gloves. Henry put together a plan to start a towing business and spent hours working on the logo until it was just the way he wanted it. Toward the end of the class, he asked if I could bring in a picture of his brother, who used to pitch for a Major League Baseball team. By that time, I'd heard a few unbelievable stories from guys who'd spent time with Mike Tyson or Jay-Z, so at first, I didn't believe Henry's brother was a former professional athlete. Nonetheless, I looked him up and learned his brother was not only a former great Major League Baseball pitcher, he'd also won some World Series games.

I printed copies of Henry's brother's old baseball cards and brought it to class. Henry appreciated my efforts and told me how his big brother had gotten special attention because of his pitching talent as early as twelve years old. In high school, his brother pitched nine no-hitters and took his team to the state championship. From there, he went straight to the big leagues, where he threw another no-hitter and was the starting pitcher in a World Series game, which he won.

I was usually careful not to ask too many questions about my student's families, but I was so caught up in Henry's story, I said one of the dumbest things in my life. "Wow, it must've been tough to try to measure up to an older brother like that."

Henry just stared as it dawned on me that trying to measure up probably had a lot to do with his situation. He was gracious, though, and just let the comment pass, shrugging and heading out to the prison yard.

The Super Bowl was the next weekend, and in hopes of trying to bring some energy to the class, I put together a book contest. Whoever picked the winning team and was closest to the point spread would win any book I could get on Amazon *within reason*. Henry won and surprised me by requesting a copy of the *Tree of Life* Messianic Bible.

"I like the way it's translated," he said. "I get a lot more out of it than I do the King James versions they have around here."

His unexpected book choice provided a good way to illustrate my prison experience and became something I used as an example when people on the outside would ask me about my students.

"They probably aren't what you've envisioned," I'd disclose. "There's no alcohol, drugs, tobacco, or women, and some of the guys get pretty spiritual. For example, the guy who won my Super Bowl contest chose a Bible when he could've requested any book available on Amazon."

Someone who seemed completely out of place with the others in G Dorm was a young white guy named Douglas. He was highly intelligent and had some good work experience that he willingly provided in class to illustrate some of my entrepreneurship principles.

Douglas put a lot of effort in, and although I never learned why he was locked up, he once told me, "They didn't like me making my own medicine." He often asked me to get him a list of books on certain subjects but wouldn't let me buy him any of them because, "My dad can afford them."

Someone told me Douglas's dad was an Ivy League professor, which wasn't too hard to believe.

Douglas put together a number of business plans, all of them forward-thinking. He brought me some articles on renewable energy and explained it would be the "next internet." About halfway through class, Douglas asked me to bring a blank business plan for a friend who wanted to start a business. I asked why his friend didn't come in and request it in person and got a vague answer. After Douglas's third or fourth request, I finally brought one in. A few weeks later, Douglas brought the completed plan back to me.

"I'll look it over," I told Douglas. "But this would be a lot easier if whoever this is would come see me in person."

"He works in the kitchen, so he can't come in during class time," Douglas explained.

I'd forgotten about the plan until a few weeks later when Douglas's friend revealed himself. A medium-build white man strolled into G Dorm wearing the white pants I later learned identified inmates as kitchen workers. As Clayton approached my teaching table, he never broke eye contact. He was a good-looking guy with cold, emotionless eyes. As he introduced himself in a soft voice, his eyes remained locked on mine. I smiled and held out my hand like a good salesman, but Clayton sort of limp-wristed the handshake with no change in his expression. I'd met my share of inmates by that time, but the way Clayton refused to break eye contact with his expressionless face seemed out of place and made me feel uncomfortable—to the point I wished there was a guard nearby.

I got to know Clayton a lot better for the next eight months or so until he was released. After learning more about him, he didn't seem as emotionless as he had when we first met. I could even occasionally coax a smile out of him, and toward the end of his sentence, he was excited about getting out and making plans to start a pressure washing business. His expressionless face was likely the defense he used in prison to keep people in check until he got to know them.

* * *

Spring had arrived at the prison, and through the tiny aluminum windows of G Dorm, I could see Kendal dutifully working his soil. It was March, so he was getting the ground ready and had compiled huge piles of mulch in the back of the garden. One morning, I went out and met him. It was truly amazing what he'd created from almost nothing. Kendal had designed the rows to work with the natural elevation of the field. He had an irrigation system of sorts in place and some early vegetables that were starting to emerge through the rich soil.

"I noticed last year that you planted late," I told him during our tour.

"Couldn't get no seeds. Begged everybody I knew to get me some seeds. They finally come through, but by then, I'd missed a big part of the growing season."

I offered to help. "Tell me what you need, and I'll get what I can."

I was teaching my class the next week when an inmate I hadn't seen before came in and told me Kendal had sent him. He handed me an envelope containing a laundry list of the seeds Kendal needed to get the garden going: bell peppers, tomatoes, watermelons, cucumbers. The list was long and precise. He knew exactly the species of each he wanted. There were notes scribbled in the margins of his list, thanking me for helping and explaining that he wasn't expecting me to get everything on the list, but any effort would be very much appreciated. He'd signed the note with a Bible verse and "Bless you and your family."

There was no way I was going to let all his hard work go for naught, so I got on the internet, found some sources for seeds, and placed my orders. When I pulled into the prison the next Thursday, I had the seeds he requested but wasn't sure the procedure to deliver them. Kendal seemed to be an honest and religious man, and he'd obviously earned the trust of supervisors at the prison, but I thought handing him a big bag of seeds without going through protocol could quickly be the end of my teaching career. Kendal seemed to come and go as he pleased; I often saw him working on projects outside the fence with no supervision. But he was still a prisoner of the state, and I'd been warned about giving unauthorized things to prisoners. I asked the guard at the gate the best way to get some seeds to the man who ran the garden.

"Kendal?" he asked. "Just take it to the sergeant's office."

The sergeant on duty took the envelope full of seeds with little ceremony and promised to get them to Kendal.

"Ain't no marijuana seeds in there, I hope," he said jokingly. Everyone at the prison seemed to know Kendal and wanted to help him.

Wasn't as big a deal as I thought.

Kendal had built a greenhouse right outside of G Dorm with some scrap wood and plastic sheeting. I could see some of what was inside from a window in the dayroom of G Dorm. Over the next few weeks, I noticed hundreds of milk cartons, cans, and anything else Kendal found that would hold soil and water with small seedlings starting to break through the dirt surface.

Kendal became one of the closest friends I made at the prison. I respected his work ethic and resourcefulness and was quick to try to give him whatever he needed to keep his operation going. I made it out to the garden when I could to see the progress. Kendal had amazing squash, cucumbers, watermelons, and okra growing in an orderly fashion. He talked about the plants as if they were children. That one had been a little stubborn, that one was doing amazing, and those over there needed some more attention. Kendal had started a ministry of sorts in the prison and used his garden to illustrate how God rewarded those who worked hard and how people could grow just like plants in the right environment.

Most of the vegetables were used to feed the prison camp, but Kendal always made sure to provide me and my wife with a huge bag of whatever he harvested. I'd frequently find a bag of assorted vegetables by my car as I left for the day with a thank-you note explaining that we were to get the "first fruits" of his harvest because we'd provided the seed.

As the growing season died down in the fall, Kendal was busy looking for another project. His release time drew near, and he was searching for a permanent place to put down roots and continue his ministry. Idlewood would be the name of his new home, and he asked me for some help in finding suitable property. Kendal gave me his specifications and the ideal acreage he was looking for and noted that a house would be nice—he could build that if needed. He wanted it to be near the prison so that he could continue his ministry with inmates or with those recently released. There was a house at the end of Palisade Prison Road he'd noticed was for sale that had a pool and some acreage, so he asked me to see what I could find out. His excitement was contagious.

I found out all I could about the house. It had been vacant for some time, which I thought could be a positive. I printed out everything I could find and left it for Kendal in our designated swap place. Two weeks later, he met me with a disappointed look as I pulled into the gravel parking lot.

"That house sold last week," he reported dejectedly.

"Don't worry about it," I said, trying to cheer him up. "We'll keep looking. If that's not available anymore, that's not the one God wants you to have."

Kendal noticeably cheered up at that remark. I'd never been one to openly talk Christianity. I was raised in a series of conservative Presbyterian churches where we typically limited the God talk to inside the church on Sundays, but Kendal's robust spirituality was contagious.

I took to my task and found three possible sites for Idlewood within a few miles of the prison. I liked one in particular. It was six acres and had a run-down house and a huge old dairy barn on the property. It looked like someone had at some point converted the dairy barn to horse stables, which would make for some fertile ground. I printed off all I could from Google Earth and real estate sites and left it for Kendal. I didn't see him for a week, but when I did, all he could talk about was the piece of land with the huge barn. He'd somehow walked the property and made an offer on it.

"We haven't heard anything back yet," he told me. "But I think God wants me to have this to start my ministry."

A week later, he owned the property and was showing me the plans that he'd drawn up from the Google Earth map printout.

Kendal sketched the whole property on a series of brown paper grocery bags. He'd drawn a place to make organic mulch, a place for beehives, a huge vegetable garden, a sanctuary, and plans to turn the barn into a wood shop downstairs and a bunkhouse for recently released inmates upstairs.

Kendal always appreciated everything I did for him, but mine was a small contribution to his master plan. Weeks later, when the deal closed and Kendal owned the place lock, stock, and oversized dairy barn, he met me in the parking lot with tears in his eyes.

"Do you remember when you said God would use you to help find me the property I needed?"

It was unlike me to say anything like that, and I had no recollection of it, but I was sure I said it if Kendal said I did.

"That's exactly what He did!" Kendal exclaimed as he took my hands and delivered a prayer of thankfulness aloud.

I congratulated him, hugged him, got in my car, and drove away. It was one of the most powerful moments I experienced as a prison teacher. Driving home, I remembered my silent prayer for a teaching opportunity on my way to the job interview a year earlier. I had no idea what I was getting into or the people I'd encounter, but driving home that day and thinking of all the people Kendal would soon be able to help with his ministry, I wouldn't have traded the experience for anything in the world.

CHAPTER ELEVEN

Riding Out the Highs and Lows

"Remember that life is full of ups and downs. Without the downs, the ups would mean nothing."

—Trina Das, educational visionary

MAYBE IT WAS THE COMPLETED class plan, but I felt confident when my fifth class started. I had more than a year's worth of prison teaching experience under my belt and was comfortable with the material and the business plan template I'd created. I was on a first-name basis with many of the guards at the prison and had multiple former students coming by the classroom to make me feel like I belonged there in G Dorm. I felt that I'd succeeded with enough of them to think I had a valid message that could, under the right circumstances, change lives by giving information and encouragement to people who needed it.

All those positive forces produced some sort of a teacher's high, which I carried with me when my next class started. My newfound enthusiasm was quickly dashed, though. With a few notable exceptions, that class made me question why I was putting so much time and effort to try to help people who obviously didn't want to be helped. The group of students also made me realize that Mr. Clean over in the programs office was doing little screening and was sending any warm body who could write their name on the class sign-up sheet.

It was the first group that took my no-attendance policy at face value and basically came and went as they pleased. I started the class with two guys who were going to be released before our graduation date, so they had no motivation to show up—I rarely saw them after our first meeting. The guys who did show were mostly polite and respectful but paid little attention to what I was doing, and few bothered to start a business plan. For the first time, I had to tell a group of students to either put away their playing cards or go play somewhere else. It seemed that I struggled every day to keep a lid on their unfocused behavior. I no longer felt like I was the business instructor at the prison, but rather babysitting grown men.

My star student was Aaron, who had good business sense and was a trained barber who wanted to open his own barber shop. He was a well-groomed dark-skinned man of about forty who sat off in the corner with a constant scowl. In our eleven weeks, I could never get a smile out of him. I couldn't decide if he was upset with his present situation or just didn't like me, but he wore a perpetual look of irritation.

I'd instituted a different case study by that time, one I put together to illustrate how a hobby could become a small business, the importance of planning, and the many pitfalls of the start-up. I found it online and tweaked it to fit the class a little better. It was about a young man who worked in a grocery store but liked to detail cars. The would-be entrepreneur found a location to start a car detailing business and considered quitting his grocery store job to go all-in on his dream. I added five discussion questions after the case study, one of which was to determine the break-even point for the start-up. That determined how much business was necessary to cover fixed costs so the potential owner could decide if his business plan was feasible. For the study, the break-even point was usually six cars per week.

It was designed to encourage original thinking, and I told everyone there were no right or wrong answers. I wanted their honest opinions and some insight. I designed the exercise with a few variables so each student was free to determine how much they wanted to charge individual customers and how much they should spend on advertising.

The case study became one of the favorite parts of my class because it brought the entrepreneurial thinkers to the surface, and the guys with the business sense were not always the students I expected them to be. Some of the quieter guys came alive and had some great insights into the best way to start and run the fictitious business.

When I got to the break-even portion, I always posed the same question to the class. "How about it? Can the owner convince enough people to get their car detailed every week? If he can't, he's not going to stay in business very long."

No one said a word for a good thirty seconds, until Aaron said through gritted teeth, "I'll go out and get the six damn cars."

"Congratulations!" I told the seething Aaron. "You've made the big entrepreneurial decision everyone who starts a company has to someday make. We can make business plans all we want, but until someone decides it's go-time, nothing happens. There are no guarantees in this, so it's always a leap of faith to some degree."

It was exactly the answer I wanted to hear from one of my students, but even my enthusiastic response was met with an angry grimace from Aaron.

An elderly Black man who sat at a table in the back eventually became a good friend. Thomas was nearing release for a twenty-plus year prison sentence and had gained some wisdom during his stay. He told me once that he wasn't going to let his family throw a party for him when he got out.

"They ain't done nothing for me while I been in here, so there's no sense doing anything for me when I get out," he explained with a serious look on his typically jovial face. Thomas was a true gentleman and one of the hardest working men in the camp. After his class graduated, I frequently saw him cleaning the guardhouse on my way in, and he never failed to stop whatever he was doing to ask about me and my family. "How's the Bulldog doing?" Thomas brightened the tiny room with his warm smile. He also did his best to keep the disinterested students in line. On more than one occasion, I heard him chide a disrespectful student during our class by explaining, "Mr. Moose doesn't have to be here."

I felt like I got into the prison environment by chance and considered it my job to provide practical knowledge students could use to keep the next set of prison gates far away. I felt like I was all alone in that quest, however. From what little I saw, the prison system in its current form did little to reform. The primary goal seemed to be to efficiently warehouse humanity and let the prisoners sort themselves out. I occasionally got to see guys like Thomas, who had somewhere along the way in his lengthy sentence decided that subservience and hard work would move him to a better place, and that taking on the system would inevitably lead to a much more difficult prison experience. While I would likely have taken the same path Thomas chose if I were in his situation, I was sure I was only seeing the small percentage of inmates who'd chosen that. The ones who couldn't or wouldn't conform would never see an honor camp like the one I taught in, no matter how many years they spent in prison.

About halfway through my fifth class, Tom, the president of the locker company we distributed for, passed through town and offered to take me to lunch. Over the course of lunch, he shared the difficulties he was having finding and keeping good labor in his locker factory. The plant was in a rural county in eastern North Carolina, which didn't have a sufficient population to staff the factory. Tom knew I taught entrepreneurship in a prison and, like a lot of people, thought it was interesting and somewhat noble work.

"Have you ever considered instituting a work release program?" I asked him.

Tom met my question with a slight look of disdain and answered, "I don't want to introduce that element to my company."

I spent the next fifteen minutes or so telling Tom what I'd learned during my time as a prison teacher. "It's not what you think. Once you meet some of these guys, you'll realize they're not bad people, just people who've made mistakes. Sometimes major ones."

He was paying close attention, so I continued with my explanation. "With work release workers, you'll get an unlimited workforce who'll show up sober, on time, and beg to work holidays. The guys make money they can send home to their families, and the prison makes money too, so they have a vested interest in the program working for you."

I apparently provided a good enough pitch to spark Tom's curiosity, and on his way out, he asked, "What are some of the things the guys did to get into your prison?"

"I get a lot of drunk drivers, shoplifters—mostly nonviolent offenders," I explained. "I've had a couple of guys who were charged with murder take my class, but they both said they didn't do it, and that's good enough for me."

He met that with a laugh and a wave as he headed out.

Later that week, I got an email from Tom. "I thought about what you said on the drive back, and we're going to investigate starting a work release program."

I eagerly responded, "You won't be sorry. Work release is

the holy grail of the prison experience. Guys pray for it, wait years to get it, and when it finally happens for them, they're highly unlikely to mess it up."

Tom did his due diligence, got the okay from the existing factory employees, and started a work release program two months later. He paid the work release people the same wage as the factory workers and gave everyone the same opportunity for advancement. Because of our conversation, dozens of men were given the opportunity to provide an honest day's work in exchange for the ability to send some money home to their families. Even more encouraging was that some former inmates became full-time workers at Penco Products.

The Penco work release program became the best result of my prison teaching efforts, and Tom always gave me credit for planting the seed in his head—truly a win-win. My locker orders shipped on time, and guys who would've been spending their time unproductively on a prison bunk had the opportunity to earn money. For some, it was the start of a career with a solid company. It all happened at the perfect time, too. The positivity of Tom's venture into work release helped to compensate for the struggle I faced with the unmotivated students in my current class.

Once Tom's program was up and running, the Greenville, North Carolina, newspaper printed a story about Penco being a second-chance employer. I sent a copy to Sarah and printed copies for my current and future classes. I would tell my students that if they weren't happy with the lack of work opportunities this camp provided to put in a request to transfer to the prison camp in the eastern part of the state to make metal lockers.

I got a call from Tom a few months later telling me one of my former students had interviewed and was working at his locker plant. The interviewee had mentioned "Mr. Moose's class at Palisade" during his interview. Tom said it took a while, but they eventually realized that he had to be talking about me and my entrepreneurship class.

My former student returned to Palisade a few months later. The job hadn't worked out, but he was happy with the experience and excitedly told me how he'd made over $400 in the week he worked there. I had him visit some future classes to talk about his experience and explain the best way to get transferred to the prison that provided workers for Penco.

As my fifth class wound down, I began to feel the physical and mental wear and tear from the long weeks catching up with me. I got up at 5:30 a.m. on Thursdays and made the hour trip to the prison to start my 8:00 a.m. class. When it ended, I'd rush back to Charlotte and work in the office until well past five, only to get up and do it all over again on Friday. Weekends were filled with typing up business plans, putting together presentations and handouts, and preparing for the next week's classes. My wife never complained, but our typical summer trips had been put on hold so I could focus on making my class the best I possibly could.

The sacrifice had been worth it to that point, but my students were just going through the motions. I didn't blame them as much as I did the people selecting them. They weren't doing any sort of interview process, but what was easiest. I canceled my guest speaker. The guy who usually came drove more than two hours to get there, and I felt like it would be a waste of his time.

As seemed to happen every time I started to question what I was doing—trying to help people who weren't interested in being helped—I got the boost I needed to stay a little longer. I met a young Lebanese man named Ali. He was in his early twenties and had a serious look about him. He ventured into my classroom one day when I was giving a presentation on using Porter's Five Forces to analyze competition and immediately took an interest. It was a huge relief to have someone who paid attention and asked questions, even if they weren't registered. It took me back to my earlier days when I had much more involved students.

After that class, Ali had a lot to say. "I've been in a lot of prisons, but I've never seen anything like what you're doing here. It's really good. Where did you get your material?"

When I told him that I'd created it from scratch, he was obviously impressed.

He said, "You gotta scale this, man. This should be taught everywhere. This is what guys in this position need to know."

"Not so much these guys," I said, taking a jab at my current group of students.

"Oh, yeah," Ali said with raised eyes, looking around at the empty classroom. "But don't let them stop you from doing what you're doing."

It was just what I needed to hear. Ali became a steady visitor and, one day, told me he wanted to start his own search engine optimization (SEO) company when he got out in about a year. Ali's sincerity and drive reminded me of myself at his age. He told me he was nearing the end of his seven-year prison sentence, which to me, meant he had likely been locked up since he was a minor.

"It's okay, though," he said. "I got a really long sentence, but I needed all this time to figure myself out." Ali somehow knew the finer points of SEO, even though he hadn't touched a keyboard in all the time he'd been imprisoned. I told him I knew little about SEO and asked if he'd put together a presentation for my class. He wrote out a series of slides free hand, which I converted to PowerPoint, and he did a great job presenting it.

For more than a year, I'd listened to constant complaints from inmates about how unfair the selection process was for getting a work release job. Some guys got it with more time to go than others, and it seemed to be a mystery to many of them how the process worked. The number one complaint was that someone who was, in their eyes, less deserving had been given a job ahead of them. I'd observed that the guys who finished my class and volunteered to work somewhere in the prison camp would quickly work their way to the top of the list. Within a few months, they'd be earning money while the guys who sat back and waited for their names to be called often waited a long time. Ali had learned how to make the most of the prison system, and in order to be placed at the top of the list for a work release assignment, he volunteered to clean G Dorm. He performed his tasks efficiently and quietly until he earned his work assignment a few months later. He was usually cleaning the G Dorm dayroom when I arrived to set up for my class, giving us the opportunity to get to know each other, and he always provided a much-needed boost to my spirit.

Ali had unlimited potential and was ready to get out and do something with his life. When I felt like I was wasting my time, he was always there to pick me up and assure me I was helping people more than I knew. His release date quickly approached, and as that day began to get closer, I promised him I'd stay until he was released because I figured as long as he was there, I'd be motivated to stay.

My fifth class graduated in early May. When the class was mercifully over and I met Richard for the graduation, my first question to him was, "What did you think of this group?"

I'd never once heard Richard say a bad word about anyone, but he hesitated, gave me a half smile, and cheerily said, "This one was different. Maybe the worst ever."

It was nothing like the earlier ceremonies. Most students seemed to be there for the big meal and the movie with minimal effort given to their business plan presentations. I started to think that maybe since I had the material down pat and had been through four classes, it was me who'd changed and not the students. The challenge was building the program, and now that I had it pretty much where I wanted it, the novelty and excitement were no longer there. I was starting to feel like I needed to find a new project.

I'd been lying low from Mr. Clean and the rest of the prison staff for months by this time. As long as I didn't venture out of G Dorm, no one paid me much attention, and I was free to run my class the way I thought best. I was about to head home from the graduation when Richard told me Mr. Clean wanted to see me in his office. On the walk over to the programs office, I couldn't think of any recent flagrant violations I'd committed, and I was pretty sure he wasn't going to give me a key to the place, so I didn't know what to expect. I waited outside his office door as I'd done before and finally was allowed entrance.

"We've been given instructions to make some changes from the state, and some of them are going to affect you," he started. "From now on, everything you bring into the prison has to be inside a see-through bag." There had recently been a prison guard killed at another North Carolina prison, and he explained that the rules were a result of that incident. Mr. Clean continued. "Also, the guards are going to be a lot more thorough in their searches from now on. Do you think you can follow these new rules?"

"Not a problem," I answered quickly and waited for my signal to be dismissed. Mr. Clean stayed hidden behind his giant computer screen, but eventually motioned his hand toward the door to signal our meeting was officially over.

I'd been using a large black gym bag to carry my teaching materials into the prison up to that point. Over the weekend, I got online and searched for clear bags. All I could find were some small youth-sized backpacks, which came complete with shoulder straps. I knew I could never get everything I needed to teach my class inside one of them, so I bought two.

It was clumsy to carry two small backpacks from the gravel lot to G Dorm every day, but I made it work, slinging the child straps over my six-foot-four frame. As for the more thorough search at the guardhouse, I never noticed anything different.

* * *

Hoping for a better group of students, I waited in G Dorm for the count to clear on an already hot May morning and watched my new class filter in from the yard. There was one white guy, Cameron, who sat at one of the back tables. He'd run a successful painting business, and his past experience and obvious intelligence were a big asset to the class. Although he mostly kept his distance from the rest, his contributions were stellar, and he was determined to get out and run his business right the next time.

"I did okay," he once explained. "But I was heavily addicted, which led to a lot of bad decisions."

That was a refrain I heard from my students frequently.

Cameron once explained that when he was nine months old, he'd discovered and ingested a lethal dose of the drugs his mother was using.

"I shouldn't be here," he told me with an out-of-place grin. "But luckily, she'd taken so much of the drug while she was pregnant with me, I'd built up enough of a resistance to it that I survived. The medics who responded to the call couldn't believe it." Cameron seemed to look at it as a lucky break, but to me, it was a horrific story.

A gray-haired Black man in his sixties sat in the middle of the room and asked me to bring him brewed coffee the first day. Mark had a polished way about him—as if he were sitting in a boardroom and not the dayroom of G Dorm.

"All we can get in here is instant" was probably the number two complaint I heard, second only to not getting work release fast enough. I thought about bringing in a small coffee maker but figured that might be pushing the boundaries and would probably lead to a lot of problems since it would never make enough to fill the demand.

As I launched into my somewhat polished "Don't break the law unless you're rich, white, and well-educated" introduction, Mark was quick to explain that he'd been forced to cop a plea for his current prison term.

"I was a badass when I was younger, and I've got two felonies from back then," he explained. "I've lived a clean life for over twenty years, man. I've got a five-bedroom house and grandkids."

Mark explained that he had nothing to do with what he'd been charged with, but his lawyer advised him against going to trial with his past record. "What's the jury going to do to a Black man with two felonies?" he posed. "So, I had no choice but to do my eight months and put this behind me."

He was obviously well-educated and expressed an interest in buying and selling real estate when he got out. He started the class with a lot of enthusiasm but seemed to lose interest as it progressed. I couldn't imagine it being easy to transition to prison in your sixties, sleeping on the metal bunks, and eating prison food when you'd had it so much better for the past two decades. My guess was that the prison experience wore him down. I saw him months later in the yard and almost didn't recognize him. He'd lost weight and looked completely defeated.

"My family's not doing too good without me there, Mr. Moose," he said. "We're gonna lose the house, it looks like."

A young Black man named Carlos sat by the table nearest the door and wanted to start a car detailing business. Carlos kept quiet until about halfway through when he took some time to talk to me after class one day. He was always smiling and seemed to know everyone at the camp. I learned Carlos's father was a pastor at a large church in a small community outside of Charlotte that also had a large private school. I knew the place well. My wife and I participated in their 5K years ago, and I'd been there over the past two summers to personally repair their lockers. Carlos had worked at his father's church most summers, mowing the yard and helping to maintain the place. Because I'd visited the church so many times, I figured we must've crossed paths at some point. His father had written a book, which I bought and read and gave to Carlos later that year. After the class finished, he became sort of a self-appointed messenger for any inmate I needed to contact or who needed to contact me. Most guys there seemed to keep to themselves or had one or two close friends, but Carlos appeared to know everyone.

The class was about halfway over when I received an invitation from Josh Proby via text. Josh was the young man who'd intimidated me on my second day at the prison with his serious nature, which I'd assumed was aggression but turned out to be determination. He'd been out for about a month and found a speaking engagement for former inmates turned authors. Josh was finishing up the book he'd told me about on my first week as a teacher and had found an opportunity to promote it by speaking to a crowd of potential publishers. Another of my former sit-in students, Anthony Williams, would also be there to promote his book, *Clerical Mistake*, and the sequel he'd completed, along with his recently designed prison publishing website.

I looked forward to seeing them. They were two guys I knew had the drive to succeed. I hadn't helped them much while they were in prison, but I respected the hell out of how they'd made their time in captivity productive. The event was held in a church auditorium near my home, and I got there early, hoping to see Josh and Anthony before it started. It was the first time I'd seen anyone from Palisade Correctional outside the prison fence. My wife was eager to accompany me. I'd been telling her about the inmates I had gotten to know for well over a year, and that was her first chance to meet any of them in person.

Anthony met us at the door, looking sharp in a well-pressed suit, much more dignified than the green and gray I was used to seeing him wear. I brought my autographed copy of his book for a quick photo session. Anthony had done a great job promoting when he was in prison. He wouldn't leave me alone until I bought a copy, and now that he was out, I knew there would be no stopping him.

Josh was tapping away on his cellphone in the back of the auditorium, wearing his usual determined look when I arrived. He broke into a huge grin when he saw me and said, "Thanks for coming, Moose."

It was an unforgettable afternoon. The audience was really into it; the emcee was lively and funny, and six authors told their stories and promoted their books. Anthony got on stage, looking much like a college professor, and told his story of false conviction, how he made his prison time productive, and even thanked me for letting him sit in on my class.

He asked me to stand up and told the audience, "I learned a lot in Mr. Moose's class. We all learned a lot."

I wasn't sure what to expect from Josh. He was scheduled to be the last speaker, and as his time approached, he was wearing out the carpet, pacing back and forth at the back of the room, looking even more focused than usual. When it was his time to go on, Josh gave a great performance. He told the story of how he and his buddies decided to rob a store one day, how the police had put down a spike strip to stop the car, and the horrific accident that resulted from hitting the strip at ninety miles per hour. Josh was able to escape the accident and make it home. He turned the news on to learn that one of his partners in crime had been apprehended. The driver, his best friend from childhood, had died in the crash.

He told us how when he first went to prison, he decided he'd be a tough guy or "wolf." His plan was going great "until I met some real wolves." His unruly behavior earned him two years in solitary confinement, providing the opportunity for some deep self-introspection. In his mandated time alone, Josh came to realize that his youthful, bad behavior was a result of sexual molestation that took place when he was a young child. He'd buried the emotions and acted out in anger to everyone around him. His time in solitary gave him the opportunity to face what happened to him and repair himself, just like weeding a garden. "You've got to get to the root and remove it completely," he explained to the spellbound crowd.

That was my wife's first exposure to the guys I'd met in prison, and I asked her what she thought on our drive home.

"You've obviously touched some people," she said. "I didn't expect those guys to hug you when they first saw you."

Explaining what it was like to teach in prison was always a challenge. It was next to impossible for someone who hadn't been there to get any sort of visual.

"Josh and Anthony are pretty amazing people," I tried to explain. "They both used their time in prison wisely and were ready to hit the ground running upon their release. I didn't do much to help either of them. They didn't need much help. But it's been a pleasure to get to know them."

Reba asked the perfect follow-up question: "You've been at it for six classes now. What's your biggest takeaway?"

I thought about it for a few minutes, trying to think of a way to explain the experience as simply as possible, and answered her question with a thought I'd not put together until that moment. "The Black guys smile a lot more than the white guys. They seem to be a lot more comfortable in the prison environment and are trying to make the best of the experience. It's a lot easier to get to know them because they're so much more relaxed than the white guys."

While we were at the conference, I met with all the former inmate authors and purchased a stack of books for the guys back at Palisade. Just like the content on the YouTube videos I brought in, I didn't think anything was more powerful to show to a man in prison than someone who'd been through the same experience, used the time they were incarcerated productively, and became successful after they got out. I gave a book from an author I met at the conference to Michael, an elderly man in my class.

He took one look at it and exclaimed, "Hey, this guy is my cousin! I didn't know they let him out of prison."

I was typing my students' business plans over the weekend and realized I wasn't giving them much feedback. After I completed each section of a business plan, I tore the sticky part off a Post-it Note and wrote "excellent" or "good job," or something to that effect, and stuck it to the part of the plan I thought was the best representation of what we'd covered in class. I assumed the student would get positive feedback and remove the sticky note so that the plan would not be marked by my comments. What I noticed after I started providing commentary was that the sticky notes stayed on the plans. That was a big positive for me. It indicated that the guys were taking pride in their work and giving credibility to my comments. I made it policy to add some sort of positive comment to each plan that was turned in each week.

I planned on finishing the sixth class as I had most of the others, with an ex-offender-turned-entrepreneur guest speaker. My usual speaker was unable to attend, but they promised to have someone meet me at the prison gate at 7:45 a.m. on our appointed date. I arrived at the guardhouse that morning and waited as long as I could for my guest speaker to arrive. When I could wait no longer, I left instructions with the guard to contact me if and when he came and headed toward G Dorm. I started my class as usual and briefly forgot about it.

About forty minutes into my class, I looked up to see an angry Mr. Clean glaring at me through the door's window. He wore dark sunglasses and motioned rapidly for me to come to the door.

"Who the hell is that in the guardhouse?" he barked angrily at me, as if I were an inmate who'd just been caught with a pack of Marlboros.

"That's my guest speaker," I explained, wearing a calm smile like it was no big deal.

"What the hell is he doing here?" he continued without toning his voice down.

"He's here to give my class a pep talk." I could tell my answer was not helping him grasp the situation at all.

By that time, we were walking side by side toward the guardhouse to intercept my guest speaker, giving Mr. Clean a good opportunity to explain how things worked. "This is a prison. You can't just bring anyone you want in here anytime you want. People have to be cleared by me." I assumed Mr. Clean was aware of the previous speakers, and I thought his outrage was unnecessary. As we walked toward the guardhouse, he seemed to be calming down a bit, and I thought my best strategy was to deflect the whole situation.

"I've been meaning to ask you when I could expect to get a key to the programs office." I threw my question out there to try to divert Mr. Clean's obvious displeasure with me.

"What key?" He glared back at me, looking completely confused. By that point, we'd arrived at the guardhouse where my Latino guest speaker was standing in a corner, looking like he wanted to go home. Instead of contacting me when he arrived, the guard on duty had called Mr. Clean, who'd instructed the guard to get my guest speaker's driver's license.

They checked his background, found out he was a convicted felon—of course—and figured we were up to no good. The situation seemed to calm down after a few minutes, and after another round of explanation, they let me bring my guest speaker in for his presentation.

I got a warning from Mr. Clean for next time, though. "I need at least two weeks' notice in the future for any more visitors," he explained. For my next class, I emailed Mr. Clean the name and driver's license number of my scheduled guest speaker, along with the day and time he'd be arriving. I never got a response and decided bringing in guest speakers wasn't worth the trouble. As much as I hated to do it, I stopped bringing anyone else in—which was a real shame since it was arguably the best part of my class.

CHAPTER TWELVE

You're Remembered for the Rules You Break

"Know the rules well, so you can break them effectively." —Dalai Lama

INSTEAD OF THE MUCH-ANTICIPATED WEEK off following the graduation of my sixth class, Richard had us starting back the next week. I hardly had time to order enough *Ice House* books or get the material together for the first meeting, but I was there on a cool November morning to start all over again.

The first one through the door was a thirty-something white guy wearing dark horn-rimmed glasses, who confidently went directly to the front-and-center table that had become prime real estate for my more motivated students. The man, Edgar, looked more like an accountant than an inmate and was quick to laugh at his own jokes with a dry, nasally bark.

I gave what had become my standard introduction: a presentation on how skewed the criminal justice system was toward punishing minorities, people of low income, and people with a low level of formal education. The presentation also included incontestable statistics, such as less than 1 percent of the US prison population had a master's degree.

As I finished the material, Edgar exclaimed, "Hey, I'm the

1 percent! I'm in prison and have a master's degree." He followed that with his typical guffaw.

I filled the presentation with as many real-life examples as I could and was always relieved when it was over. I was fully visible on the prison surveillance system, bashing the justice system and encouraging the inmates to think they were there largely due to their life's position—not their crimes.

About halfway through my "criminal justice system is rigged" slideshow, a guard entered G Dorm, took a seat in the back, and watched with interest. It was common for a guard to wander through during class, and a few stood by the door to watch what we were talking about on occasion, but that was the first time one had taken a seat. I wasn't going to let it deter me, though. The first time anyone tried to censor my material was going to be my last day as a prison teacher. The guard got up and left after I finished the presentation, but came back when I was packing up and asked me to bring him the sources for my unfair justice system statistics. I wasn't sure if he was asking out of self-interest or to use it to report me to his boss, but I was confident that handing him a printout of my slideshow wouldn't end well for me. He asked a few more times over the weeks that followed, but I never delivered them. Giving the presentation was worth the risk, and they could run me out of there if they wanted. But I wasn't going to give them the rope with which to hang me.

A couple of guys from earlier classes frequented my seventh class. I always left the door open and encouraged it. They were a positive presence and would hopefully show the new class there were reasons to come other than the twenty-seven days reduced from their sentences and moving a notch up the list for work release. Carlos, the man who seemed to know everyone at the prison, was one of the regulars.

When we took our first break, Carlos walked up with a smile so wide his eyes were slanted shut. He was a close friend of Josh and knew I'd recently seen him at the ex-offender-turned-author convention.

"How did Josh do at that thing you went to?" Carlos asked excitedly.

"He gave a great speech," I told Carlos. "And he's finishing up his book."

"I sure would like to see that speech, Mr. Moose. Any way you could bring it in?"

I promised to see what I could do and told him I'd contact Josh to see if anyone had recorded it. Josh, a great self-promoter, beat me to the punch and posted it a few days later on his Facebook page. It took a few tries to get right, but I was able to download it and burn it to a DVD. When I returned to prison the next Thursday, I told Carlos I had a copy of Josh's presentation and would show it the next day during our 9:30 a.m. break.

As we neared our break Friday, G Dorm started filling up with inmates. Some I knew, and some I hadn't seen before. The typical inmate did his best to look intimidating, and having the room fill up unexpectedly put me on edge. Carlos had spread the word, and Josh had obviously made a big impression during his incarceration. To my surprise, some of the third-shift work release guys rose from their bunks and sleepily entered the room, which became standing room only.

"I'm guessing you guys want to see Josh's presentation?" I stated the obvious, trying my best not to look uncomfortable. I thought it was best to call the 9:30 a.m. break a little early and get the growing crowd what they wanted before one of the guards came in and broke it up. No one from the class left the tiny dayroom, and it fell completely silent as the grainy Facebook copy of Josh's presentation started on the two small TV screens. After it was over, no one left, so I played it again. Carlos was beyond excitement by that time.

"Not everyone who wants to see it is here," Carlos said.

"Could I have a copy of that DVD to show in the chapel tonight?"

I realized giving a DVD to an inmate was probably way out of bounds and thought back to my instruction of "Give them class material only, then take it all up before class ends." I was way beyond that, though. I'd given the guys hundreds of notebooks, pens, and books relating to the businesses they wanted to start.

As the inmates who came to the Josh Proby show silently filed out of G Dorm, I handed Carlos the DVD, which he quickly slipped into the front pocket of his oversized green yard jacket.

"Thanks, Mr. Moose." Carlos gave me one of his world-class smiles and disappeared out the front door.

Ali, who was quietly watching the proceedings from the back of the dayroom, came up to me with a troubled look.

"You can't do that, man!" he said, obviously concerned. "You can't give guys like him stuff like that. It all has to go through channels. They'll reprimand you big time for doing that." Ali had become a good friend and confidant and had my best interests at heart. He was a true believer in what I was trying to do there and had seen me stretch boundaries along the way, but I'd crossed the line that time—he was quick to let me know.

"If it costs me my job, it costs me my job," I told him. "I have to tell you it'll be worth it. I can't think of anything I can do to help these guys more than to show them an example of someone who was in this prison less than four months ago and is now on the outside making something of his life."

Ali shook his head and looked at the floor. "You just gave them all they need to get rid of you," he said.

I knew Ali was right, and I started to regret that I'd let Carlos's exuberance cloud my judgment. I'd been a prison teacher for a year and a half by then and knew a big part of my job was getting guys to believe in themselves. Many had been a part of a system designed to beat them down for so long it was becoming part of their identities. I wanted to make it possible for everyone in that camp to see how far Josh had come in such a short period of time in hopes that they'd be encouraged to do the same. If I couldn't make them believe in themselves, then all the business instructions in the world would be worthless.

"Here's the thing," I told Ali. "I'm not here for the paycheck or the teaching experience anymore. I'm going to do whatever it takes to try to help the people I can while I'm here because one day, they're going to come and escort me out of here. I've already accepted that."

Ali's bewilderment started to change a little as he considered my perspective. I was halfway kidding, but I was always going to be on thin ice in the prison environment. There was no way I would conform to what anyone else thought I should or shouldn't do. At the same time, I never really expected to be escorted out of G Dorm.

Josh knew I was going to show his presentation that morning, so when I was driving from the prison to my day job, I gave him a call.

"We had a full house," I told him. "Standing room only. I had to play it twice for everyone."

Josh wanted to know who all was there, but I only knew the guys by their given names. He knew them mostly by their nicknames, so our attempts to meet on the common ground of descriptions nearly needed a translator.

It went something like this:

"Billy was there."

"What's he look like?"

"Tall guy, dark hair. I think he's a Lumbee Indian."

"Chief? Chief was there?"

"I think so."

Despite the success of the morning's presentation, I owed it to Josh to let him know what I'd done with the DVD.

"I might have a problem, though," I explained. "I gave Carlos the DVD of your presentation to show in the chapel tonight and was told that it could get me in a lot of trouble."

Josh fell silent on the other end. After he thought about it for a minute, he responded, "Don't worry about that, Mr. Moose. I'll make some phone calls. You don't have to worry about that."

Josh knew some of the higher-ups at the prison and had been back on a few occasions to give motivational speeches. I knew he'd smooth things over for me if he could.

I'd been going at it really hard for the past year and a half. I was driving home on Fridays absolutely exhausted every week, and my weekends were spent almost entirely on preparing for the next week's classes. I had guards going through my bags on my way into the prison and had never been given a key to the programs office, access to the computer system, or permission to park where the other instructor parked. After talking to Josh, I felt like I had some support for the first time. Ironically, it did not come from a prison authority—it came from a former inmate.

A light-skinned Black man with thinning hair and a lizard-like stare sat in the front row of that class. I don't think I ever saw Lucas in a bad mood or at a time when he didn't seem to be enjoying every minute of the day. He'd worked for his father's lawn mowing business so, appropriately, he was putting together a business plan for a lawn care service. His experience provided some great classroom examples. His father would charge five dollars to mow yards—a ridiculously low price—but he'd pick a neighborhood and mow just about every lawn in the subdivision.

"It costs next to nothing to mow one more yard once you're

already there," Lucas explained. "And nobody could beat our price."

I always discouraged a low-ball pricing strategy when we got to the pricing portion of the business plan. Instead, I encouraged them to charge a premium and provide a high level of service because I believed it was one of the keys to survival among start-ups and small businesses. I had to give his father credit, however, for his low-price strategy, which took advantage of the economies of clustering his customers. I wasn't going to let Lucas get off that easy, though.

"In your business plan, try to think of some services you could provide existing customers that they'd be willing to pay a little more for," I challenged the incessantly smiling Lucas.

About halfway through the class, he asked me to do some research on a hotel in his hometown that he heard might be for sale.

"That might be a good opportunity when I get out," Lucas said.

I couldn't find any information on the hotel he was interested in, so I found some photos online of the most run-down hotel I could find and put them on a slide deck. Then, I waited.

A few classes later, Lucas asked, "Were you able to find out anything about that hotel?"

"Glad you asked," I told him as I scanned through my list of presentations. "I did find some information."

As the pictures of the boarded-up hotel that was just about to fall in on itself hit the screen, Lucas knew instantly that I was setting him up, but he was quick to join in on the fun.

"That's it all right, Mr. Moose. It looks a lot better than I remember." He beamed.

"I think we can fix it up in a few days once you get out, no problem," I prodded.

Edgar, who was always ready for a laugh, piped in, "Maybe

instead of digging all that sand out of the pool, you could open it as a sand spa." He followed that with his trademark honk.

The rest of the class was completely oblivious to the gag. "That looks like a lot of work to me," someone in the back said in a confused tone.

It was rare to have that perfect mix of chemistry to introduce any sort of humor into my class because I was always overly careful to not call anyone out or make them feel uncomfortable. Egos, I learned, were often very delicate in a prison setting, and being disrespectful to anyone was potentially dangerous ground. Lucas was one of the rare guys I taught who I knew could handle having a little fun without taking any offense at what might have otherwise been considered disrespectful.

One student I was never sure I could joke around with was George. He was a young, quiet white guy who might've said six words the entire class and became terrified toward the end when I told everyone they had to give a presentation at graduation. George reminded me a lot of myself in my undergraduate days, sitting as far away from the action as possible and contributing little or nothing. He met me at the gate the morning of our graduation, and we had our only conversation.

"I had a death in the family last night," he stammered. "It's been really tough on the whole family, and I won't be able to give my presentation today."

I knew he was lying and usually wouldn't let someone off that easily, but George appeared completely terrified.

"You're good," I told him. "Sorry to hear about your family situation."

When he realized he was off the hook, his all-encompassing nervousness instantly vanished, and he quickly paced ahead of me in the yard toward the graduation ceremony, careful not to give me a chance to change my mind.

I learned a lot from George. I thought he was doing the bare minimum just to get the time off and to gain favor from the prison staff, but I later realized I misjudged the situation. After he graduated and my next class started, George became a regular visitor to the G Dorm dayroom. He was the first one in the door and always sat in his same seat. He continued to keep to himself and rarely said a word, but his attendance spoke volumes. I looked back on the instructors that had been a positive influence to me as a student and how, just like George, I never said a word or gave them any sign of appreciation. Seeing it from the other side helped me realize that I might be accomplishing a lot more with my teaching efforts than what was obvious to me.

The seventh class would be remembered as the class of the future truck driver. Of the ten guys who started the class, three of them wanted to drive long-haul trucks. Trucking was something I recommended early in every class to guys who couldn't develop a start-up business idea because the industry was desperate for drivers. The young guys didn't like the travel, and the older guys don't like being watched by cameras in the cab or being tracked by GPS. It was possible to start working on the docks and work your way up to a full-time semi-truck driver, which could lead to being your own boss. I had some YouTube videos created by ex-offenders who worked their way up the ladder from the loading docks and now owned their own trucks.

Some trucking companies overlooked criminal records, including felonies, and paid for truck driving school in exchange for a two- or three-year commitment to drive for them. It was a good move for someone with a checkered past, and I purchased a book on Amazon that served as a primer for the commercial driver's license exam. The book cost around thirty dollars, more than I got paid per hour, but for a guy who seemed earnest in wanting to change his future, it seemed like a small investment. I bought three of them for that class.

"I'm working for free today because of the cost of these books, so don't let me down," I told them as I handed them out.

I sort of hated to see that class end. Edgar put together a solid business plan to purchase portfolios of old consumer debt and hire former inmates to do the collecting while taking advantage of numerous tax breaks along the way. He had a strong knowledge of information systems and was confident he could put together an algorithm to help him sort out the collectible from the non-collectible debt. My future truck drivers seemed focused and ready to do their own thing when they got out. Even the quiet guys were respectful and got along with everybody. The chemistry was good, and I wasn't sure what awaited me the next time, but that class gave me the strength I needed to move forward and take on one more.

* * *

I never got a role sheet for my eighth class, which was a mix of ages, races, and learning abilities. Walking through the yard on my way to our first meeting, I met a heavily tattooed white guy who matched my six-foot-four height, but was probably fifteen years younger. Travis had a perfected prison swagger, indicating he was completely comfortable in his environment. He stood out in the yard as if he were expecting me and stared at me with a steely glare. I felt like he was testing me to see if I would look away first. His accent was mill-town-North Carolina nasal, and he was quick to tell me he was serving his sixteenth prison sentence. Travis explained he was taking my class and followed me from the prison yard to G Dorm, taking his place at a table in the back of the room and entertaining me with a story of how he'd once lost more than $100,000 in a few hours in an Indian casino, all while I set up my equipment and waited for the rest of the class.

As the room filled up, he loudly informed me that he

wouldn't be around for graduation day because he'd been locked up for a parole violation and had only two months to go.

"I don't know what I can get out of your class since I'm not going to be able to finish it," he challenged.

"I'll try to make this worth your time," I shot back. My comment caused a quiet chuckle from Ali, who sat at a front table and shrugged to show me he also wasn't quite sure what to make of Travis.

Many of the guys in that class took me up on my "If you can find something better to do than come to my class, do it" challenge. They started disappearing from the first session. Besides Travis, I had two other guys who would be released before graduation pull quick exits. Of the guys who bothered to come, there was little interest or interaction with my material. The lone bright spot was a dark-skinned young guy named Marlon, who had great start-up ideas. Every week, he had a new one, unique and elaborate. He started with crime scene cleanup, which we learned was billed hourly and covered by insurance.

"I've got a strong stomach. That stuff doesn't bother me," he explained.

His next business idea was to wash semitrucks at truck stops with a pressure washer. I thought that was a great plan because it had almost no start-up costs, and I wasn't alone. Marlon's plan got Travis's full attention.

"Oh, now that's something I can do," Travis proclaimed after Marlon shared his newest plan. "Trust me, I can make that work." Travis, never short on confidence, had been given a plan and was focused on bringing it to life.

Unbeknownst to him, Marlon saved the class. He was released a few weeks in, but before he left, I bought him a blank notebook with "Big Ideas" printed on the front and told him to keep track of everything he came up with. Sooner or later, he was going to hit it big.

Even so, that class gave me more thoughts of ending my prison teaching gig. It was obvious that having a pulse was the only prerequisite Mr. Clean considered necessary for taking it. To complicate matters, he was filling the class with guys who'd be released before our graduation date. Of the ten guys in that group, three wouldn't be around long enough to finish, so they had little incentive to attend. I could understand their logic. What got me through was not the registered students, but the few non-registered guys who attended regularly and were interested in doing something different from crime when they got out. They thirsted for the knowledge that could get them there.

One of those guys was Gabriel. He was a skinny, dark-skinned Black man who wore the telltale white pants of a kitchen worker and had a pointed goatee, piercing eyes, and a ready smile. I learned his brother owned and operated a small construction business, and Gabriel had worked for him in the past and thought his brother wasn't running it properly. He wanted to learn about the right way to run a business so that he could help his brother upon his release.

Gabriel was quick to ask if he could sit in on my class and had no problem asking questions to slow me down when he felt I was going through the material too quickly, a challenge I continually faced. Because my typical poker-faced students didn't provide much in the way of visual feedback, it was difficult to gauge how well my material was being received, and because I didn't formally test on what I presented, I often wondered how much of what I'd worked so hard to put together was absorbed.

Gabriel was a welcome presence. He seemed familiar with the prison ways, and by the looks he sometimes gave me, I got the feeling he thought the material I presented and my habit of handing out books and notebooks was nowhere close to standard prison protocol. Like me, Gabriel would enjoy it while it lasted.

After we got to know each other fairly well, Gabriel asked if I could write a letter of recommendation to his parole officer for his upcoming parole hearing. I'd never been asked to do that before, but I wrote a letter explaining that Gabriel was a welcome presence in my class and was working hard to gain skills that would help him on the outside, even though he was getting no time off or any special favors for his efforts. Gabriel seemed to appreciate the letter. He stopped coming toward the end of my tenure there, and I asked Ali if he'd made parole.

"That guy?" Ali asked. "He's got a life sentence. I don't think they'll ever let him out." I wondered why a guy with no exit date had been so focused on my class material and so sure of his future. More than anything, I missed having him in class.

By then, I'd been a prison teacher for sixteen months. The early Thursday wake-up call seemed to be coming a little faster each week, and my weekends were spent unpacking teaching material from my clear backpacks, updating business plans, creating content for the next week, and cramming it all back in the tiny backpacks Sunday night. The eighth class put all my efforts to the test. I came home one Friday evening dead to the world and complained to my wife about the students who were exiting my class en masse.

My wife, who'd encouraged me every step of the way through all my educational pursuits and my teaching job, looked me over and said, "You know, you're going to have to give up your teaching job before it does you in."

It was the first time I'd ever heard a discouraging word from her about any of my extracurricular activities. Deep down, I knew she was right.

Christmas provided me with a much-needed week off, but then we were back at it for seven straight weeks until graduation. With four weeks to go, the class decreased to five guys. Travis, the habitual felon and future truck washer who'd not missed a single class, was nowhere to be found. As the class progressed, I looked out one of the windows and noticed him mowing the grass with a push lawn mower. Friday came, and Travis was out there again mowing over the same spot as he had the day before. Combined with all the frustration I felt with the class, I was irritated. I had put a lot of time and effort into helping Travis with his truck washing business plan, and when we needed his voice in the class the most, he was out mowing the lawn.

What angered me the most was that, despite his sometimes daunting appearance, Travis had a natural ability to make people like him. He was always honest, from what I could tell, and could turn on the charm when he wanted. With his abilities, I believed he could start a small business and make it work. That was consistently the most frustrating part of my job—when I cared more about a student's future than they did.

I had numerous conversations with Travis outside of class and thought we had established a level of mutual respect. Up to that point in my prison teaching stint, I'd learned to tolerate students who missed classes or made a minimal effort and had instead focused on the people who appreciated what I was trying to do. On that particular day, my frustrations—at Travis, at the class, at the system—boiled over.

"Well, there's a student who takes my class seriously," I told my remaining four students as I nodded out the window toward Travis, who obliviously passed by G Dorm, pushing the same mower in the same place he had just twenty-four hours ago. "It might not be so bad if he hadn't cut that exact same place yesterday, and it's unlikely we've experienced a whole lot of turf growth since then."

I got a few raised eyebrows and smirks from the smattering of students in the dayroom. I probably should've kept it to myself, but enough was enough.

Word travels fast in prison, and shortly after I called for our 9:30 a.m. break, I saw an angry-looking Travis glaring in through the square plexiglass window at the top of the aluminum door. When I first took the job, the absolute last thing I wanted was to have a disagreement with an inmate, but by that time, I didn't care anymore. I was physically and mentally tired and looking for a reason to quit. I'd proven myself among most of the inmates as a fair guy who had their best interests at heart. Travis had single-handedly upped the stakes. He'd chosen to perform pointless labor instead of showing up for class, and he was doing so right in front of me.

"Do me and you have a problem?" Travis strutted through the doorway and made a beeline for my corner table. Like most of the guys at Palisade, Travis could be physically intimidating if he wanted to be. He was over six feet tall, had tattoos all over his arms, a split tooth, and a razor-sharp glare. He knew his way around prison protocol. I'd seen him make other inmates clean what he'd established as "his" table if they were sitting at it when he entered the class and he didn't like the way they'd left it. They all sheepishly complied. I knew that calling Travis out like I did was going to get back to him, and there was no way he was going to let me say something about him behind his back without holding me accountable.

"We do," I said. "I need you in this class. We're down to five guys now, and isn't learning how to start and run a truck washing business going to serve you better in the future than cutting the damn yard?"

I wasn't too worried about a physical altercation. The guys who made it to the camp seemed to all know better than to do anything but have short verbal disagreements with each other—at least that was all I'd ever seen—and Travis was down to some short time. I was pretty sure he wasn't going to punch out the teacher and miss his chance to go home.

"You don't understand, Mr. Moose," Travis explained firmly. "I'm here on a parole violation, and I've only got twenty-three days to go. If I cut the yard, I get time off my sentence. So, if they ask me to cut the yard, I'm going to do it. And if they ask me to cut the same patch of grass every day until they let me out of here, I'm going to do it. I've got to get home to Momma, man."

"Look, Travis," I relented. "I appreciate your situation, and I'd probably do the same thing if I were in your shoes, but do me a favor."

"Whatzat?" he asked quizzically, raising an eyebrow and looking ready to shoot down whatever I was about to ask.

"When you get home, I'm counting on you to give your business idea a try. You have the smarts and the personality to pull it off."

Travis's forceful demeanor instantly changed as his shoulders dropped, and he managed a tight grin. "You know I will, Mr. Moose." Then, for good measure, he added, "You know I will."

Toward the latter part of my teaching career, I walked a fine line between feeling like I was supposed to be there and wanting to pack up my material and go home. It seemed that every time I mentally got too far into either of those extreme mindsets, something would pull me back toward the center. With just a few weeks to go in a class of dwindling and unmotivated students, an inmate I knew named Patrick walked into my class from the bunk room one Friday morning, which wasn't an unusual occurrence. Patrick was a tall bearded white guy who'd sometimes sit in on my Friday class since he worked Monday through Thursday at his work release job. Patrick ran a construction business years before and, like a lot of guys at Palisade, had an addiction that destroyed his personal life and eventually landed him in prison.

On that Friday, Patrick walked out of the bunk room at about 9:20 a.m. with a stern look and loudly interrupted my class, "About time for a break, isn't it, Moose?"

"Not yet," I said, confused as to why he'd interrupt my class that way. It seemed way out of character for Patrick, who'd never been my student but had always been respectful. Patrick usually talked to me with a smile, but he wasn't smiling that morning. He stood over in a corner with his arms folded, staring at me and waiting for me to announce the morning break. I looked around the room, and it seemed that the few guys remaining in the class heard Patrick say the word "break" and were in the process of packing up and heading out the door.

"I guess you're right, Patrick. It *is* break time," I said, still not sure what had changed his friendly demeanor but knowing I was about to find out. He seized the opportunity to march straight at me with an atypical all-business expression.

"Good. Because I've got some questions for you, Moose."

I'd been there long enough to learn some guys had bad days. Guys had shown me divorce decrees they'd unexpectedly received in the mail, and I witnessed a few tears in the programs office on occasions when they got bad news regarding something that had happened at home or with a family member, so I tried to give the inmates a lot of room regarding their occasionally unpredictable behavior. My time in prison was limited to a few hours a week. I had no idea what it was like to be there for years. I couldn't imagine what had come over Patrick, though. I knew him well enough to know he was taking correspondence marketing classes and, one time, had shared a joke with him about an escape attempt when I encountered him repairing the back gate. He'd seemed to be a predictably calm person, someone who wanted to do what time they had left and put the whole prison experience behind them. I stood my ground as he approached, ready for just about anything.

"Why weren't you at the volunteer dinner last night?" he asked, remaining steadfast.

I'd seen something about volunteer dinners they had once or twice a year to show appreciation for the people who donated their time at the prison, but I never thought they applied to me.

"Well, I get paid to be here Patrick, so technically, I'm not a volunteer," I explained. "I'm employed by the college."

Patrick shot back, "Well, Mr. Moose, because you weren't at the dinner last night, we couldn't give you what we made for you to thank you for all you do for us."

With that, Patrick handed me a handmade wooden clock with a carved moose standing prominently in front of a mountainous backdrop. Etched into the wood were the words, "I Moose Not Forget!" which I recognized from one of my many moose-appropriate notepads I'd used to leave notes for Kendal the gardener. Scripted at the bottom was "From all your Friends at Palisade Correctional Center."

Patrick's serious demeanor quickly changed to a friendly one, and he seemed to enjoy that he'd put me on the spot before giving me the gift.

The gift was completely unexpected, and if some of the guys were looking for a way to show their gratitude, it hit the mark. I knew some of the inmates appreciated the amount of work I was putting in to try to help them improve their lives, but for them to put the time and effort into a personalized symbol of recognition meant a lot more to me than I could express. I took the clock from Patrick and felt a lump in my throat. No way was I going to get emotional in the prison dayroom, though. If Patrick was aware of my masked emotional reaction, he didn't show it.

He was back to his old smiling self by that time and added, "You've really helped a lot of us here, and we want to thank you for that. A couple of the guys were up all night making this, but they can't be here because they're working, so they asked me to give it to you."

The clock hangs proudly on my office wall, keeps good time, and serves as a reminder of the hundreds of guys I encountered during my prison teaching stint. Like a lot of the good things I was lucky enough to be a part of at the prison, it wasn't what I expected.

It was much better.

* * *

Graduation day came for the group, and of the four students left from the original ten, only one made any effort to complete his business plan. Instead of the usual round robin "Tell us about your business plan" presentations we used to start the day-long graduation ceremony, I told my overachieving student if he didn't want to get up and talk, he didn't have to. I would've been embarrassed as an instructor to only have one student out of ten with a completed business plan. I thought it would be better to put that class in the past.

As Richard and I cut the vegetables for his famous graduation salad, I took the opportunity to vent a little bit about the students we'd been sent. "If a guy knows he's going to be released before our class is completed, how are we supposed to motivate him to learn the material?"

Richard, I had learned, started working at the prison as a guard more than twenty years ago. When he learned the local college was looking for someone to teach commercial cleaning, he applied for the job and had been teaching for almost ten years. He had a great rapport with everyone at the prison and was not one to complain about anything.

"We'll just hope they do better for us next time," he said. "You get some good classes, and you get some bad ones."

This bad one had me rethinking my teaching future altogether. Again.

CHAPTER THIRTEEN
The Slow Boil

"The future is inevitable and precise, but it may not occur. God lurks in the gaps."
—Jorge Luis Borges, Argentine short-story writer

I DROVE AWAY FROM PRISON that day in February 2019 thinking I'd give it one more chance. The schedule Richard created provided me with two weeks off, which was most welcome. I celebrated by taking my wife to Savannah, Georgia, to run a half marathon, providing an opportunity to both think about my situation and draft a letter of resignation to the college when we returned home.

My plan was to find out how many students in my next class would be released before our scheduled graduation. If even one of them wasn't going to be there long enough to complete the class, I'd let the college know that would be my last one.

The ninth class would run through September 2019, which would give me almost two-and-a-half years of classroom teaching experience—the minimum requirement for most of the other teaching jobs I'd seen posted. It seemed like a good time to make a lateral move before I became typecast as a "prison" teacher. I initially experienced a huge thrill from finally landing a teaching job, spent many hours learning what my students needed and the best way to deliver it, and had built a one-hundred-hour curriculum from scratch. The shine had dulled, though, and I was physically tired and frustrated with the caliber of students. The two-plus years had been a roller coaster of highs and lows and, sort of like exploring an unchartered cave, had mostly taken place in the dark. I had no way to see what was around the next corner until I'd already turned it.

My two-week break passed quickly. I ordered enough *Ice House* books and wide-ruled notebooks to accommodate the ten new students, plus whoever joined us from the yard. I loaded my two clear book bags with eight hours' worth of handouts, DVDs, and thumb drives with "Week 1" material and headed to the prison in the darkness of 6:30 a.m., ready to call it quits at the first sign of a possible absentee student.

I noticed upon arrival that, in my short absence, there'd been a procedural change. All inmates who were not sleeping off the previous night's work release assignment in the bunk room next to my classroom were lined up around the basketball court, sitting directly in front of G Dorm. I'd seen that type of assembly twice before when drugs had been found and the head of the prison, "Mr. Porter," paced back and forth on the court and berated the entire camp. This was different, though. In an effort to expedite the inmate counting process, someone decided it was a lot easier to count the prisoners if they were all in one place, which gave me the opportunity to see a lot of guys from previous classes I otherwise wouldn't have seen. I took my time and traversed the court, talking to whoever made eye contact and seemed affable.

With the exception of rainy days, that was the new counting procedure for my remaining tenure.

On that morning, count cleared, and my ten students gradually trickled into the classroom. I began again. An elderly white man, Larry, took front and center, along with a forty-something Black guy whose reserved smile set him apart from the typical inmate. Lou was well-groomed, overly polite, and seemed genuinely happy to be there. It was obvious he and Larry were good friends, and I got the feeling Lou had taken the older man under his wing and was looking out for him.

A large, dark-skinned Black man took the table by the window. He gave me a passing glance and spent most of the first class looking outside with a bored expression. I eventually learned his name was Jeremy, and he had once run his own hot dog stand, which I hoped would give me a source for small business experience—always a welcome resource to illustrate classroom concepts. It became clear, though, that Jeremy was not one to socialize. He came in by himself, stayed in the dayroom through break, and left by himself.

A thirty-year-old white guy with dark wavy hair chose a seat in the middle of the classroom, introduced himself as Spencer, and quickly informed me he had no interest in learning anything about cleaning, but Kendal, the man who ran the garden, recommended he take the class to learn the business essentials. Spencer was never afraid to contribute and once told me about all the businesses he'd started.

"I could always sell whatever I was doing at the time, but I was just trying to make enough money to feed a serious addiction, so it never went anywhere," he explained.

So far, so good. I had two guys with possible business experience and two more who seem focused and mannerly. Maybe I wouldn't be sending in my resignation letter after all. I decided to learn my fate, and after some brief introductions, asked if anyone would be released before the class ended in early September. No one responded except an elderly white guy with a gravelly smoker's voice who'd chosen a seat at the table all the way in the back.

"None of us is going anywhere any time soon," he volunteered.

I was encouraged to think that I had been given a good group of guys to work with.

Looks like I'm in for at least another eleven weeks.

Approaching my two-year anniversary as a prison teacher, I'd created a twenty-eight-page guide, which was a constant work in progress that outlined the material I'd use in each class from start to finish. PowerPoint presentations were highlighted in brown, handouts in yellow, DVDs in purple, and my *Ice House* chapters in an appropriate icy-blue color. That was the backbone of the course, but I'd interject examples from businesses the guys planned to start and always tried to spend time looking at the competition in their desired locations.

The challenge of determining the best material for my class had long ago been completed. I was now mostly tweaking it in the necessary places and upgrading the bland parts. I was where I'd wanted to be—no longer spending weekends scrambling to figure out how to fill the ninety-nine classroom hours one week at a time; the fear of running out of material before I ran out of class time was long gone. Instead of putting the class on cruise control and enjoying the ride as I'd planned, I was becoming bored with the repetition. Just like the locker company that had taken me over two decades to build, I'd put my class together the way I wanted, and the thrill was gone. Maintaining what I'd already built provided no joy to me. I was ready to move on and build something else.

Although I was starting to seriously look for an exit strategy from my teaching job, the first few weeks of the class went well. Coincidentally, the pastor at the church we attend delivered a five-week series on finding spiritual purpose, which hit home for me. I wrote a letter to the pastor, thanking him for a great series and informing him he'd convinced me to continue as a prison instructor even though I'd prepared a resignation letter weeks before.

The class seemed to sail through my early material outlining what entrepreneurship was, the advantages to starting their own businesses, and why former inmates could make great entrepreneurs. As we started to decide which business each student should start, I introduced a concept I learned in my MBA program: a SWOT analysis. The process consisted of identifying the strengths and weaknesses inherent in a planned or existing business, and also the opportunities and threats that existed in the environment and location in which they planned to open.

To illustrate the SWOT analysis, I assembled a PowerPoint on businesses my typical student would be familiar with, starting with McDonald's restaurants. McDonald's was usually good fodder for a classroom discussion. Everyone had had a good or bad experience, or at least an opinion on how they stacked up compared to other fast food restaurants.

As I prodded the class for some strengths and weaknesses of the McDonald's operations, the man by the window, who'd mostly been sitting silently until this point, awoke and began to contribute. It turned out Jeremy had once managed a McDonald's and knew the business inside and out.

"You put your best people on the drive-through," he explained. "We called them 'aces and faces.' They handle most of the business and have to be fast and accurate."

As Jeremy continued to explain how to run a McDonald's, his whole demeanor changed. He was engaged, smiling, and obviously enjoying himself. Maybe it was the excitement of remembering a better time or being the local expert on the topic, but Jeremy's passion was contagious, and before long, the whole class was alert and conversing. Together, we had a great hour-and-a-half-long discussion on the McDonald's way of doing business, including what the organization did right and wrong.

"How important is it to McDonald's to be a kid's restaurant of choice?" I asked.

"You never let a kid have a bad experience," Jeremy explained. "If you see a kid crying, you hand him a free ice cream cone."

"That was awfully nice of you, Jeremy," I said.

"Doesn't have nothing to do with me. That's what they taught us to do. Kids bring their parents in, so we always tried to keep the children happy."

That discussion turned out to be an anchor for the class. Maybe it was because remembering a trip to McDonald's made the guys feel normal for a while or some sort of connection we all felt to McDonald's that cut through our pasts and current situations to bond us as a group, but things changed that day. We became a unified group, and the chemistry stayed strong over the remaining weeks.

When it came to deciding their business plans, Spencer decided he wanted to start a pressure washing business, and I found a whole series of YouTube videos created by a guy who started and ran a successful one. It was great material; the entrepreneurial pressure washer had included a how-to guide you could get from his site by providing your email address. I downloaded it for Spencer and received an email from the pressure washer the next day asking where I was going to start my business. I responded with an explanation that I was downloading it for an inmate who planned to start one upon his release from prison.

He responded, "God bless you. Keep up the good work, brother."

In that class, I had four main students who remained engaged. Jeremy somehow did independent research on investing in Fortune 500 companies, bringing them to class for me to copy and hand out. Spencer was my newly gung ho future pressure washer.

Lou followed me to the gate one day, and in a perfectly delivered sales pitch, asked, "Mr. Moose, how would you like to hire a guy who can go out and get some of those big locker contracts for you?"

I was a pushover for a good salesman, and Lou had it down—steady delivery, good eye contact, welcoming mannerisms. He knew what he was doing.

I'd decided the day I took the job that I wouldn't make any promises about anything on the outside. There was no sense in giving them misguided hope, and it seemed like a long shot that any of those guys would expect me to hire them.

"Wish I could," I told him. "But we've got everyone we need right now."

"Okay then, Mr. Moose." Lou used the same consumer behavior principle, contrast, I taught in class: start by asking for something big, and whatever you ask for next will seem much smaller by comparison. "We'll just get together for a steak dinner, then, and see what we can work out."

"That we *will* do," I promised. "I'm looking forward to that."

With a big smile and a firm handshake, Lou turned and walked proudly through the prison yard, obviously pleased that he'd closed his big deal.

About halfway through each of my classes, I covered risk management. It was part of the business plan, and I felt it was important to outline some of the risks inherent in a small business start-up. People were the risk at the top of my list. My philosophy had always been to treat the people who worked for you a little better than they expect to be treated, which I had learned years earlier in an organizational behavior class. To get and keep loyal employees, you should pay them a little more than they can get anywhere else for doing the same job. Also, doing small, unexpected favors goes a long way to making them devoted to your cause. I learned early in my locker career that keeping the office refrigerator stocked with an employee's favorite brand of soda went a long way toward making them feel appreciated.

For that part of each class, I preached that efforts taken to reduce employee turnover always pay dividends. An ex-employee who goes to work for your competition takes over what you taught them, also taking the equity you invested in developing them. An even worse scenario is an ex-employee who starts his or her own business to compete with you, taking some of your customers with them. After I delivered that advice and called for a break, Lou eagerly approached my table with a story of his own.

"I think I did what you just talked about in my business, Mr. Moose." Lou was obviously excited to have made the connection between his real-life experience and my class material. "Let's say I asked you to drive for me one day, and you pick me up at eight o'clock in the morning." As Lou began his story, his eyes widened, and his words emerged faster. "I might say, let's swing by Hardees before we get started, and I'll buy you breakfast. That's something you didn't expect from me, and like you said, it's a small thing, but it might be big to you that I was being thoughtful that you might not have eaten breakfast that morning."

"Exactly!" I agreed. "It's the small things that usually go a long way."

Lou wasn't finished, though. "Now, I have them drive me to Walmart and wait outside in the car while I go in and get a grocery cart." Lou was using hand gestures, getting more animated by the minute. "What I do is head right into the bedding department at Walmart and fill my cart with all the king-sized sheet sets that I can fit in it. I don't get the queen-sized sheets or anything smaller because those sizes are hard to sell. Next, I get some laundry detergent and put it underneath the cart, and I'm good to go."

I had no idea where Lou was going with his cart full of king-sized sheet sets and laundry detergent, but he quickly filled me in.

"Now, I've got to get past the security at the front door and get out to the parking lot as fast as I can, and my driver pulls up and helps me load all the sheets and detergent in the trunk of the car." His eyes grew larger as he explained the final detail. "Those sheet sets sell for $75 in Walmart, and I can get half that, around $40 a set, selling them door-to-door all day long." He hesitated and let the brilliance of his business plan soak in before he continued. "If I hit any resistance from my customer, I offer to throw in a bottle of laundry detergent for free since they're going to want to wash the sheets before they sleep on them. By the end of the day, after I've paid my driver, I usually would have somewhere between $300 and $400." Lou's eyes glazed over as he finished his story. "What do you think of *that* business plan?" he asked me with a burst of pride.

His story had taken an unexpected turn—outright theft—and as much as I enjoyed hearing it, I was at a total loss for words, unsure whether to praise or condemn his illicit doings. Lou was completely unfazed by my silence, though; he spun on his heels and strode proudly out of G Dorm like he'd just explained to me one of the great secrets of the universe.

Part of the material I used for my risk management topic was an extracurricular classroom exercise or what I referred to as our class field trip. As I reviewed the syllabus on the first meeting of each class, I always briefly mentioned there'd be a class field trip. That seemed to get, at the very least, some raised eyebrows from my new crop of students. Richard would occasionally take students out of the prison to clean a church or state-owned building as part of his class, so the guys knew it was possible to leave the camp. It felt like a somewhat cruel gesture to tease them too much about it, so I always provided the details to anyone who seemed to be getting too worked up over the possibility of leaving the prison. I typically left it with, "We're not going far, but we are leaving G Dorm."

I'd borrowed the idea from an entrepreneurship lesson plan while I scrambled to find content before starting the teaching job. Their version utilized a trash basket and wadded-up paper. Students scored points every time they tossed a wad of paper in the trash can. Point values were agreed on before the exercise. The farther shots were worth more points than the closer shots. Students were split up into teams, and each team member was given two shots. They could start at any point value they wanted, with the rule being if they missed the first shot, they could only move up and take an easier and less point-worthy shot. If they made the first shot, they could shoot from anywhere they liked. The purpose of the exercise was to illustrate the relationship between risk and reward. The less risky shot had a lower point value, but a greater chance of scoring. A good strategy was to take an easy shot for the first shot in order to get some points on the board, then take a riskier shot for a second shot, especially if your team was ahead.

I originally thought of using a trash basket and paper wads as spelled out in the lesson plan, but realized because we had an actual basketball court at our disposal, we could play the game in a much better arena. The class field trip provided a way to get everyone out of the classroom and participate in an activity as a group. It was a great way to involve the whole class while illustrating a core concept, and it provided us with a way to have a little fun.

When it was time for our field trip, I explained the rules late on a Thursday afternoon and let the guys decide the point values of each shot in hopes of getting them to take some ownership of the exercise. In my earlier classes, I divided the teams up randomly, but in later classes, I gave a risk management assessment to each student and divided the teams according to their risk tolerance, just to make it interesting. Before I dismissed them, I told them we'd take our field trip around 9:15 the next morning and that the winning team would go on break, while the losing team would have to return to G Dorm to take a test I'd created on class material. I was conscious of providing any material objects for the winning team and thought the best way to stay out of trouble was to reward them with a break.

That was my ninth class, and I'd never asked to use the court before. I'd learned it was better to ask forgiveness than permission, especially in a place where everyone seemed primed to shoot down all my requests. I had no problems using the basketball court for my first eight classes. Guards would sometimes come by the court, curious as to what we were up to and possibly relieved an instructor was using the court with his class since it was usually off-limits during that time of the day.

I sent them out to warm up for the exercise while I copied down the agreed-upon point values and team rosters, as I'd always done in the past. After a few minutes, Jeremy rushed through the door to the dayroom, wide-eyed.

"You better get out here, Mr. Moose. They don't realize we're using the court as part of your class."

Before I could make it out the door, the sergeant got on the PA system and emphatically instructed my students to get off the court. I walked over to the programs office and knocked on the door. After a few minutes, I got someone there to answer and call the sergeant for me—I still had no key and no idea how the phones worked.

I apologized to the sergeant for not asking his permission

but explained that it had always been part of my class and asked if it would be okay to use the court.

"Okay, but let us know next time," he replied sternly.

I recognized the voice on the phone. The sergeant for that day was an older guard I'd previously had a few conversations with—he seemed to be an okay guy. Although I thought it was unusual to clear the court over the PA system like that, I wrote it off as a misunderstanding.

Jeremy had a different take on the situation, and he seemed to know a lot about how things worked in prison. After his team scored the winning basket, he followed me back to G Dorm.

"They're getting a new attitude around here—lots more rules and regulations than there used to be."

Jeremy saw a lot more than I did, and I was in no position to doubt him. It seemed out of character for the sergeant to be as rule-oriented as he'd been with me, but I'd never had any problem using the court in the past and didn't think I would in the future.

The overall mood at the prison did seem to be changing, though. I saw only a very small part of the picture from my corner of G Dorm two mornings a week, but guards who used to stop and talk to me during breaks or before class would walk through the dayroom without making eye contact, and the new procedure of lining the guys around the basketball court for morning count seemed a lot less solicitous than the old method of counting them on their bunks.

As the class wound down to the final weeks, my students again began to disappear. Lou had been given a job as an emcee for the prison play and missed a lot of classes for rehearsals. A local church paid for a two-day self-improvement seminar to be streamed into the prison, which happened to coincide with my Thursday and Friday class on my penultimate week. Word got around that the seminar normally cost $109 per person, which gave it a lot of perceived value to the inmates, and they packed the chapel to watch. I couldn't blame them for taking advantage of one of the few resources that had been offered to them, but I spent two days teaching a skeleton crew of students while the rest of my class sat in on the seminar.

As the end of the class approached and graduation loomed, Gabriel, my outside student from the kitchen, began questioning whether he'd be part of the graduation ceremony. That was always a tough question to answer. Richard had no way of knowing who sat in on my class and didn't see any of my non-registered students until graduation, so he had no idea who had contributed or worked up a business plan. I had zero authority as far as who could be at the ceremony, so I hated to promise anything to anyone no matter how much the guy deserved the recognition.

I answered Gabriel like I'd done previously to my other sit-in students: I'd try to make them as big a part of the party as I could, but I couldn't guarantee anything. My wife would make extra brownies, and because I bought the fried chicken with my own money, I made sure there was plenty of it so that the unregistered students wouldn't be empty-handed. On more than one occasion, they moved the graduation to the smaller side-pocket room where my job interview had taken place and wouldn't allow anyone not officially in the class inside to watch the movies or share the food due to a lack of space. That led to some frustration for me and some obvious displeasure from the guys who'd put forth a good effort and weren't allowed any of the rewards. The graduation party was a chance for them to eat food from the outside world, watch first-run movies, and enjoy themselves for half a day. I hated to see those who contributed and built business plans be denied the celebration because fun days like that were rare inside the prison fence.

Gabriel had attended my classes for several months, asked

good questions, and put together a solid business plan for an existing business his brother started. He worked in the kitchen and was always apologizing for showing up late or leaving early, but he had responsibilities in other parts of the prison. He was a solid contributor, and his continual presence turned a lot of mediocre classes into good ones. I wanted to include him in the festivities as much as possible. I got busy during the graduation and didn't see Gabriel for the whole first half of the morning, figuring he'd either been turned away or had responsibilities in the kitchen that were preventing him from attending. He came in about halfway through the party, after we'd almost finished our meal. Another student, Sam, was quick to inform me Gabriel was there and that we should've put aside some food for him.

Sam was an elderly white man who was registered in the class but hadn't said much for the past eleven weeks or even started a business plan, and I didn't think he noticed Gabriel's classroom contributions or efforts. Sam was obviously disappointed in me for not putting some food aside for Gabriel, and he went to work, rounding up some spare chicken, salad, and dessert, presenting it to Gabriel as if we'd been saving it for him.

Gabriel was obviously appreciative, and when I went to thank Sam, he gave me a look of bewilderment and scolded me, "He was an important part of our class. I don't know how you could've overlooked him like that."

That surprised me. Sam and Gabriel appeared to be from two completely different worlds and had never had a conversation I was aware of, but Sam went out of his way to be sure Gabriel wasn't overlooked. I was used to guys staying in their safe circles or keeping to themselves, so it was refreshing to see the consideration of one inmate to another, despite their likely differences.

* * *

Richard made some changes to the schedule so he could take two weeks off in November for a Caribbean cruise. Instead of the usual week off I always enjoyed, we started the next class with no break, and although I would have enjoyed the time off, it was just a matter of ordering enough notebooks and *Ice House* books and bringing in my "Week 1" material for the next week.

The first guy through the door on day one was a young Black man named Arthur. He took the seat directly in front of my teaching table. Arthur had some experience working for a small electrical company and had his electrician's license. He was all business—first one through the door with no time for small talk. He was there to learn and mostly sat expressionless throughout the entire class.

Two elderly Black men took the back table farthest from the door. Jacob was a gray-bearded man from a nearby county who often nodded thoughtfully along with my presentations. He initially struggled with a business idea until he remembered how local museums would call him when they needed a snake. My first thought was that he was buying and selling reptiles, but Jacob put me straight.

"I can catch any kind of snake there is," he said. "Any time the museum needed one, they'd call me, and I'd go find one and bring it to them. It paid pretty good, too." Based on his experience and unique skill set, Jacob thought he might do well starting a critter control company.

His tablemate, Carl, was a tall, skinny Black man who wore one-size-too-big prison-issue clothes and gray dreadlocks. He always had a bemused look on his face, which I assumed meant he was surprised they let a guy like me through the gate to teach. Sometimes, after a lengthy or high-level presentation, he shook his head and looked at the ground, gesturing like he couldn't believe what he'd just heard. I could never decide what his mannerisms meant, but he seemed to always be enjoying himself and was overly nice and respectful.

Three white guys decided to share the table in the far corner next to the door. That table was so far away from the front of the classroom that it was impossible to see what was being shown on the small TVs. In previous classes, it sat mostly empty except for the occasional inmate who wandered in from the yard to observe my class for a few minutes or to write a letter.

I started the class with my "Don't break the law unless you're rich, white, and well-educated" presentation and threw down my standard introductory challenge.

"I don't take attendance, and if you can find something better to do, do it."

Instead of taking that as a challenge, the three white guys sitting as far away from the action as possible took it as an invitation to ditch my class from that day forward.

The brazenness of them taking my challenge at face value irritated me initially, but after the first few weeks, I thought that maybe they'd all been transferred or had found something better to do, which was okay with me. I didn't want anyone to be there who didn't want to be there. I had enough students making an effort and typically had a few from the yard come in and fill the empty seats. Because I never got a roll sheet for that class, I forgot about my absentee students after a few weeks.

When we started the risk management portion of class, I stopped by the sergeant's office on my way in and asked the shift sergeant behind the desk if I could use the basketball court that morning for a twenty-minute exercise.

When I first began teaching, my first stop at the prison was the sergeant's office since it provided the only bathroom that I counted on not being locked. During that time, I had gotten on a first-name basis with some of the guards who worked there. About a year into my teaching stint, a convenience store opened along my route to the prison, so I began stopping there to use their restroom instead. The visit to the sergeant's office that morning was my first in months.

From what I could determine, the sergeant was a rotating position. There seemed to be different guys in charge at different times. I once asked if I could park a box truck from work in the gravel lot so I could make a locker delivery after class, and the elderly sergeant of the day was accommodating.

Over the years, I'd made a friend with a guard whose last name was Hill. He was a big, jovial guy who invented a tabletop game he planned on making and selling to local taverns. As a small business instructor, he kept me posted on his progress throughout my time there and eventually built a few working prototypes of his game, which he test marketed with some of the inmates.

On that particular morning, the sergeant on duty was a younger white guy in his mid-thirties who wore army combat boots and tinted glasses. I'd seen him around, but he wasn't the type of guy I'd try to chat up. He walked with overstated authority and liked to look intimidating.

I explained that I'd used the basketball court for a class exercise for every class since I'd been there.

Hill, who was behind the counter, was quick to say, "If it was up to me, it would be fine."

But that wasn't the answer I got from the man in charge. "Not a good idea," he said. "If other inmates see you out there, then they'll think it's okay for them to be out there too, and the court is off-limits until eleven."

Noticing my annoyed look, he added, "I tell you what, if you want to go out there at ten forty-five, that would be okay."

That really hit me wrong. "It's got to be nine fifteen. The winning team takes a break, and that's our break time," I tersely explained.

"Well, I guess you're out of luck then," the sergeant shot back with a wave of dismissal.

"Thanks a lot," I said as sarcastically as I could and walked out, noticing Hill's surprised look.

It seemed like another turning point. If nothing else, it put me in a bad mood for the rest of the day. I explained to the class that the exercise had been canceled for no good reason and watched out the window as their fellow inmates played on the basketball court the entire morning.

Even from my limited exposure to the pulse of the prison, that typified the overall mood change. When I started as an instructor, the prison appeared to be a relaxed place—at least as relaxed as I could expect a prison to be. The guards were mostly helpful, or at least cordial. I asked to use the basketball court only out of politeness, and I thought it to be a minor request. I got the feeling the sergeant told me no solely because he was in a position to do it, and that he enjoyed the power to deny my request.

I had another run-in with the same guard a week later when I was passing through the guardhouse on my way to class. He asked for my credentials, and I snapped back that I'd never been issued credentials and had been entering the prison for almost three years without them. I could tell he didn't like my response or the way I said it. Those were guys who were used to doing and saying what they wanted with no back talk. He glared at me through his tinted glasses and waved his hand toward the gate without another word. We never said anything to each other from that point forward but exchanged steely glances when we crossed paths.

I didn't know what had changed or why it had changed, but the run-in with the guard didn't seem like an isolated incident. I could detect a change in the overall mood of the staff. Guards who used to talk to me on my way in and out of the guardhouse kept their eyes on computer screens and were non-conversational. The inmates were pretty much the same, but when I complained to Jeremy about not being able to use the basketball court, he had a knowing look about him.

"That's how it is in here now," he said.

Jeremy was right. Something had changed.

Because Richard was taking his two-week cruise, the class ran for thirteen weeks instead of the usual eleven. We got to week five when Carl came up to me during a break and complained about the injustice of the three no-show students getting certificates for completing the class and enjoying all the trimmings of the graduation celebration without making any effort.

"How is that fair?" Carl demanded.

I did my best to get him to see things from my perspective.

"Look, Carl, I see your point, but I think we're better off without them. The certificate is just a piece of paper. What we're learning in here are things that can improve your life when you get out. If they don't want to learn them, I'd rather they not take up the space for the people who do."

Carl wasn't buying it, though. He shook his head and sat down with an incredulous look.

I had some time to think about our conversation, and I decided to make a policy change. I designed my class to be non-traditional, but those guys were flaunting my no-attendance policy. I thought it might be a good idea to give them a wake-up call. The next day was a Friday, so I told Carl privately before class that if he wanted to tell the three absentee students I was starting to take attendance, I'd back him up. He got a mischievous grin on his face and slipped out the door during our 9:30 a.m. break to spread the news.

Sure enough, one of the three, Rick, came in during the break with an angry and anxious look on his face.

"You said you weren't taking attendance, and now I hear

that you are." He was an older guy with gray hair. He was probably older than me, which was rare in my classes.

"You signed up for the class, so you need to be here," I told him. "What else do you have to do anyway?"

Rick was quick to show his displeasure. He shuffled back to the distant table he'd chosen on day one and glared at me as he sat.

I figured I had nothing to lose at that point, so I decided to call him out when the class got back from break. "We're talking about health savings accounts today or HSAs. Do you know what they are, Rick?"

He shot me a pissed-off look and a shrug.

"They're savings accounts that provide a place for you to put money tax free. You can spend this money on healthcare for you and your immediate family in just about any way you choose," I explained as nicely as possible. "As a bonus, they allow you to provide very good health insurance for your family at a low cost, or possibly for free, and provide you with an avenue to invest money so you never have to pay taxes on your gains. Does that sound like something that could make your life and the lives of your family better?"

Rick was staring out the window at that point and had no reaction. I could make him show up under the threat of taking attendance, but there was no way to make him give a damn.

Carl was all smiles, though, soaking in the moment he helped create. I felt more like a kindergarten teacher than an entrepreneurship instructor that day, and I was never sure that going back on my attendance policy was the right thing to do.

The students in that class were not big on participation. There were two Black guys who sat in the middle of the room who put forth an effort but rarely said a word. One of them, Dante, sat in silence for the first half, then started to open up about halfway through the course. He was a dark-skinned man in his thirties with wide eyes and usually wore a sullen expression. His father had recently passed away and left him a house that was paid for in a nearby town. Dante asked me to check and see if the property taxes had been paid on the property. I did a Google search on the address, and the first link to pop up was a front-page story about a big drug bust that had taken place at the house a year and a half ago. The story had a photograph, and they had blurred his face, but there in a lawn chair on the front porch sat Dante with his hands cuffed behind his back.

Although we came from different worlds, Dante and I had a somewhat similar past. I learned from him later that, just like my dad had taught me the locker business, his dad had taught him the illegal drug business. They were different businesses, but I could sense some of the same pride I had when Dante would talk about his father's distinguished business acumen and the discipline it took for him to pay that house off.

I tried to encourage him to get into real estate when he got out. Because he already had one house paid for, I urged him to consider leveraging it to buy another one nearby. If he could find a good fixer-upper and put some sweat equity into it, he could either rent it out or flip it and begin his journey as a real estate mogul. He seemed to take an interest in the plan. I ordered some books on real estate investing and house flipping and told him to take advantage of what his father left him. When the class started, Dante was mostly unresponsive, but by the time I left, he seemed to be excited about a possible future as a landlord.

"I'm not going to tolerate anyone using drugs on my properties," he told me one day. "It just leads to trouble."

Quite a turnaround.

I got so little interaction with students over the next few weeks that most days I felt like I was talking to myself. My efforts to draw them out were largely unsuccessful, although

I received a lot of smiles and nods. The guys were in no way hostile or disinterested—they just didn't have a lot to say.

Ali would regularly sit in on the last few minutes of my class and help me pack up. He was a welcome presence with his consistent smile and handshake. We would spend a few minutes catching up and, on occasion, I would tell him it seemed like I'd spent the last three hours talking to myself.

Ali always provided some level of encouragement, like, "Hang in there, Mr. Moose. You're doing more good in here than you know."

He was scheduled to be released June 1, which was only a few months away. I felt my teaching career was likely drawing to a close, but I told Ali I'd stay at the prison and continue teaching until he was released. As had become typical, every time I planned on giving up the teaching job, a good reason to stay would present itself.

CHAPTER FOURTEEN

Turns Out, They're Crooks Just Like Us

"Justice cannot be for one side alone, but must be for both." —Eleanor Roosevelt, former first lady

THE TENTH CLASS WAS SCHEDULED to graduate the second week of December. With only a few weeks to go, I arrived, as usual, at the prison early on a Thursday morning. Everything seemed fairly normal as I wheeled into the gravel parking lot and selected a choice parking spot next to the dumpster.

My first clue that something had changed was when I entered the guardhouse and noticed the walk-through metal detector had been turned on. The guardhouse was such a narrow building that there was no way to make it from the entrance to the door that led to the prison yard without walking through the metal detector. I'd been passing through it for almost three years without paying it much attention, but the yellow lights blinking for the first time that morning signaled it was operational.

I looked quizzically from the metal detector to the guard who sat reading a newspaper at the nearby desk and asked, "Do you need to watch me walk through this?"

The guard never looked up from his newspaper and slowly

answered, "It don't matter. We can't figure out how to calibrate it."

The detector screeched as I walked through it, carrying my two clear bags containing a variety of teaching material. The guard never flinched, so I kept going and exchanged the usual pleasantries with the guys I knew surrounding the basketball court.

Class began normally. I started a motivational DVD presentation to the silent crowd and took my seat at my corner table. After my introductory presentation, and as I was about halfway through my first slide, Dante started making eye contact with me and tipping his head to motion for me to walk to the back of the classroom where he sat. His interruption irritated me, so I ignored him as long as I could. When a student needed to talk to me, they'd typically get up and approach my table. I could think of no reason why he expected me to come to him.

Dante persisted with his eye contact and head waving until I finally stopped what I was doing and grudgingly walked over to where he was sitting.

"Mr. Moose," Dante whispered with a raised brow. He spoke so quietly I could hardly hear him. "Mr. Moose, I gotta tell you something."

I didn't understand the drama, so I stood directly in front of him and answered with a loud and annoyed, "What?"

Dante partially covered his mouth and said in a low voice, "Porter's gone."

Porter was the stocky bulldog of a man who was the head of the prison. I'd been at the prison almost three years, and we'd never said a word to each other. Porter was laser-focused on the inmates, and I was not his employee nor his problem. When there was trouble at the prison camp, like someone on work release testing positive for illegal drugs, Porter's modus operandi was to line the entire camp around the basketball court and pace back and forth in front of the inmates while telling them how bad their lives were about to get. He'd made an unexpected appearance in one of my early classes and forcefully taken one of my students away after shaking down his books and papers for contraband. He was a man with a tough exterior, which got him respect among the inmates, and the kind of guy you wanted to be in charge of a prison.

Dante enjoyed my surprised look and quietly added, "Ms. Roberts—she gone, too."

I had no idea who Ms. Roberts was, but I was starting to understand something *big* was happening.

"Mr. Kemper ain't here no more either," Dante concluded with a mischievous look.

Kemper was pissed-off Mr. Clean, the head of programs, and one of the only two people in the prison I'd known since my interview.

I wasn't sure why I was being told so secretively, but I figured Dante didn't want to be seen spilling the beans on one of the G Dorm cameras. Because Dante and his fellow inmates probably knew best, I softly replied, "Wow, what happened?"

"Don't know much," Dante said out of the side of his mouth. "But I heard some money's missing."

Word spread quickly in the tightly contained prison environment, and although the rest of the class couldn't hear what Dante was saying, they knew what the message was and met my inquisitive look with solemn nods. They seemed to enjoy that someone besides them was in trouble for a change.

About ten minutes later, an announcement came over the PA instructing everyone to assemble immediately in the chapel for an important meeting. The announcement made it clear that everybody meant *everybody*, including the sleeping guys who worked third shift the night before.

Through the window, I could see the entrance to the chapel across the basketball court from G Dorm and watched as the inmates began shuffling through the gate. I wasn't sure if I should join the group. I didn't work for the prison and had no stake in whatever was going on, but curiosity got the better of me, so I went and said hello to a bunch of former students I hadn't seen in a few months. The inmate population had packed the chapel to the point that it was standing room only, so the long adjacent hallway held the overflow. I found a place along the crowded wall in the corridor and stood next to some former students. Everyone was abuzz over the big shake-up, and I heard at least three different theories as to what might have happened. At the front of the room were three people I recognized from the programs office: two men and a woman. They stood at the front as a group and looked out of place and uncomfortable. They obviously hadn't had time to rehearse their presentation.

The woman spoke first. "As everyone probably knows, as of yesterday morning, three of our senior staff members are no longer working here. We're going through an unexpected transition and need your patience and understanding until we can get everything back to normal."

Instead of Porter's toughness, her approach was a request for patience and compassion. That type of tonality would've been more appropriate for a group presentation at a shareholders' meeting. It was completely out of place in a prison chapel full of convicted felons. The incarcerated men seemed to quickly recognize the feebleness of her message. You could almost feel the balance of prison power tilting slightly askew the longer she spoke.

The next speaker said more of the same in the same tone, then opened the floor for questions. An inmate I didn't recognize raised his hand and asked why the basketball court wasn't open in the morning anymore, then another asked if anything could be done about the meager lunch portions he'd been getting lately.

While the three people from the programs office were busy dodging more unrelated questions, I decided the inmates had taken control of the meeting and exited back to G Dorm to beat the flow that would soon be pouring out of the chapel. Minutes later, the work release prisoners were passing through the dayroom on their way back to their bunks. In my two-and-a-half years at the prison, I'd never heard them so loud before. They sounded like a victorious basketball team returning to their locker room after swishing a buzzer-beater.

I knew my friend Ali could enlighten me on the situation, so I caught up to him on my way to the gate and asked him for his insights into the recent events.

Years ago, the prison had put together a traveling inmate quartet. I remembered Sampson telling me he was in the group and how much he enjoyed traveling to different churches to sing God's praises and the great restaurant meals that followed. I thought it odd at the time that a convicted murderer with no exit date was leaving the camp, but because everything was new to me, I brushed it off as my unfamiliarity with the prison system. Sampson didn't seem to be a violent person, but he did have a life sentence with no parole. He was so strong that if he'd decided to make a run for freedom, it would've taken more than one guard to restrain him.

Apparently, the traveling inmate quartet sometimes got love offerings from the local churches and revivals, and from what Ali heard, the money hadn't been accounted for. Some senior state prison officials got word of the traveling vocal group and investigated who was paying for the restaurant meals the singing inmates received after their performances. When the Palisade prison staff could produce no accounting for the trips, an inquiry was launched: computer hard drives were seized and at least three people were forced into early retirement. None of it was ever substantiated to me, but I heard from numerous sources the amount of money missing was in the neighborhood of $50,000.

Ali was extremely observant and had been in the prison system for a long time.

"It never looked right to me," he explained. "Taking these guys in state-owned vans all over the place to work the revivals and church services. Sometimes, they'd be gone for a long time. I don't really care about that, but things like this can change the whole climate of a prison. I've seen it happen."

I told him I thought the tone of the meeting in the chapel would've been more appropriate if given by a CEO to a room full of shareholders rather than by prison officials to wards of the state. I also told him about the loud voices and the celebratory tones of the men returning to G Dorm after the big meeting.

Ali explained, "There are going to be some changes here as a result of all this, let's hope they're good ones."

I drove back to Charlotte, reflecting on all that had happened that day and thinking about how quickly things could and would change. Students and ex-students I'd gotten to know over time would suddenly be gone with no explanation. My efforts to find out what happened to them were always met with resistance. No one seemed to know much about what happened to other inmates or where they ended up—or at least they weren't talking about it.

"He got moved" was about the most detailed answer I ever received. Similarly, the head of the prison and the head of programs were gone overnight with little fanfare. In my experience, it was rare to get to say goodbye to anyone in the prison environment. One day, they were just gone without a trace.

The next day, Friday, November 15, started as just another day to get up early, head to the prison, and start my class. I was so isolated from the prison politics that I didn't think any of the staff shake-up would affect me. I'd never even met Porter and hadn't seen Mr. Clean in many months before they were both sent home for good.

I made my usual stop for coffee at the nearby convenience store, grabbed my clear bags from the trunk of my car, and headed toward the front gate. As had happened a few times before, a box truck was making a delivery of refrigerated food through a side gate in front of the small guardhouse; the temporary opening in the fence would allow me to bypass the front gate. There were two inmates unloading plastic crates of milk and other dairy products onto a cart when I arrived, so I asked the guard who was watching the side gate if it was okay if I came through his gate rather than going through the trouble of going up and down the ramp to the guardhouse. He nodded his approval and motioned me to go through the gate, so I expeditiously entered the prison yard. Before I could take more than a few steps, frantic tapping rattled the guardhouse window.

I looked up to see the guard stationed inside frantically motioning at me through the small window to come in. The guard du jour was a young white guy I'd gotten to know fairly well. I didn't know his name, but he seemed pretty easygoing. He must've learned through the prison grapevine that I taught investing principles in my class because he stopped me one morning months before to discuss some of the stocks he owned, also wanting to know what I thought of his choice of mutual funds.

That day, he sported a semi-panicked look and was in no mood for small talk. I gave him a congenial wave and headed up the steps to the tiny guardhouse, looking at him inquisitively as he stood in front of his small desk.

"I can't let you in without credentials," he told me with a tense, uncomfortable expression. "That's the new rule. No one gets in without credentials."

I'd been through that a few times before, so I thought nothing of it. I wasn't a prison employee or volunteer and hadn't been given any credentials over the previous three years. Until then, I'd always been able to talk my way out of their requests.

"The only thing I bring in here is my car keys," I explained. "But I can go out to the car and get my driver's license if that will help."

"No." The young guard looked away, agitated. "You've got to have credentials that show you've been cleared by the state to be in here."

"Well, I don't have them. I've never had them, and I've never needed them before," I countered.

"I'm sure you know what's been going on here," the young man responded in a calmer voice. "We're in the process of an ongoing state investigation. We've got some new people in charge now, and I've been given instructions to not let anyone in without the proper credentials."

We were at a stalemate, so I decided to attempt to push through the red tape since my class was going to be starting momentarily.

"Here's what I'm going to do," I said. "I'm going to go down to G Dorm and start my class because my students are probably already sitting there waiting for me. I'm going to go straight there, and I'm not going to leave G Dorm until my class is over. And then, I'm going to come straight back here. You can watch me on cameras the whole time, and because I don't have a key to any door in this place, I can't do a whole lot of harm between now and when my class is over."

The guard didn't reply, but I could tell by his stance he wasn't sure what to do.

"If you want to have this conversation after class, we can have it then, but now I've got to go down there and get started before students start wandering off."

The young guard sat down at his desk with a defeated look and turned his back to me. I took that as my cue to get out of the tiny guardhouse and went out the door, down the stairs, and through the gate that led to the prison. I was running late and would have to set up my equipment with the whole class watching, which was not how I liked to start.

I hustled up the ramp to G Dorm and was greeted by seven or eight students from the class, along with a few students sitting in from other classes. Levi, a student from my third class who took the time to greet me every morning, sat up front, and Jeremy, the McDonald's manager from my previous class, was sitting about halfway back. Cole, an intelligent dark-skinned young man with thick glasses who sometimes sat in on my class and had shown an interest in real estate investing, was sitting at the table with the view of the garden. I'd ordered a book for Cole on house flipping that had come in the day before, and I dug through my bag until I found it and handed it to him on my way to my corner teaching table.

"Thank you," he said, surprised. "I'm going to use all this stuff when I get out."

"I know you will, Cole," I assured him. "I have no doubt you're going to be successful." In my time spent as a prison teacher, I learned that information was best served with a side of confidence. Cole gave me a nod of appreciation as I scrambled to unpack my small bags.

Due to my background in sales, I considered being late to an appointment inconsiderate of whoever was expecting me, and I preached the importance of being on time to each of my classes. In my almost three years of teaching, I'd only been late to class once—and that was due to a traffic accident that shut down the only road leading to the prison. Every eye was on me as I hurriedly walked to my table and began unpacking the DVD player and VGA wire.

"Apologies," I told the seated men. "We had a hold-up at

the front gate this morning, but I think I was able to clear that up. We'll get started as soon as I get this hooked up."

It took me a few minutes to get the DVD player plugged in and to run the wires through the splitter to both TVs.

By then, I had nine classes under my belt and created a large assortment of motivational DVDs that I would use to start each Friday class. I usually decided over the weekend how I wanted to start and would put the DVD front and center in the case where it would be easy for me to find. Sometimes, I picked two and selected the one I wanted to show when I got to the prison, depending on the mood of the class. Occasionally, I left the house unsure which was the best DVD to start with, but I always had a plan by the time class started.

Not that day, though. It was the only time in almost three years that I totally drew a blank. I pulled out the DVD case and began mindlessly flipping through. Nothing looked right. Nothing felt right.

Suddenly, it didn't matter. The young guard from the guardhouse entered G Dorm and, in an authoritative voice, told me that the sergeant wanted to see me right away. He got the full attention of my students, who were used to that type of treatment, but not accustomed to it being directed to an instructor. I put my DVD case down and followed the young guard out the door. He walked with me stride for stride as I was sure he'd done hundreds of times with inmates. We were about halfway to the guardhouse when we crossed paths with one of my current students who was running late.

"You going to the hole, Mr. Moose?" he asked with a bemused expression.

"Doesn't look good for me right now, does it?" I shot back with raised eyebrows, enjoying his joke. I was sure I was going to meet the guard who wouldn't let me use the basketball court, Mr. Tinted Glasses himself, back at the guardhouse. I was ready to give him hell. I figured it had a lot to do with the icy glares we'd been giving each other. I was still annoyed at him for canceling my basketball court exercise, but being escorted out of my class was the last straw. We returned to the surprisingly empty guardhouse and waited for the sergeant of the day to strut through the door.

While I stood there waiting, I kept looking down at my watch and back at the young guard, trying to make him as uncomfortable as possible for wasting my time.

After a few minutes, I said, "I thought the sergeant wanted to see me."

"He should be here any minute," he replied nervously and quickly got on the wall phone to find out what had happened to the sergeant. He was unable to get an answer and started uneasily explaining his actions just as he had on my trip earlier that morning. "They've assigned a temporary warden to this place, and he told us this morning that no one gets in here without state-issued credentials." With an apologetic look, he said, "I'm just following orders, man. Maybe I shouldn't have stirred all this up."

I waited another ten minutes, then decided that wasting my time was a premeditated power play by whoever was in charge. It was time to leave gracefully before the situation got heated and I said something I'd regret later—or worse.

The silence stretched on. "Here's what I'm going to do," I finally said. "I'm going back to G Dorm. I'm going to pack up my teaching materials, and I'm going to drive back to Charlotte. When you figure out what credentials I'm supposed to have and how I'm supposed to get them, you let the college know, and maybe I'll come back."

He seemed okay with my plan and opened the door that led to the prison yard. I could hear a lot of raised voices as I walked up the ramp to G Dorm, but when I opened the door, the twelve seated men fell completely silent.

I wasn't sure if it was going to be my last day as a teacher or not, and even though I was angry, I didn't want to make a big issue out of all that had transpired. I had survived so far in the environment by staying out of the politics, showing up, doing my job, and going home. I quietly disassembled my DVD set up and began packing my two clear book bags. I would occasionally glance up at the room full of guys who were silently staring at me and waiting for some kind of explanation.

"I've got some really good news for some of you." I stared directly at Rick and his otherwise empty table. "No class today. You're all free to leave."

It had been a frustrating morning, and I was in no mood to be courteous to Rick and his band of no-shows. I figured they got exactly what they wanted. Rick stood up, not sure if I was angry or trying to be funny, and quickly exited the dayroom via the nearby door.

No one else left the room or made an attempt to get out of their seats. They all sat staring at me, waiting.

"I can't be in here because I don't have credentials." I looked around the room briefly and added, "The reason I don't have these credentials is that they don't exist, and I've never needed them before in the almost three years I've been coming here."

I looked around the room, waiting for some sort of reaction, but everyone sat frozen, waiting for me to continue. I wasn't sure what to say next. I wasn't going to bad-mouth the young guard. For all I knew, everything would all be cleared up, and I'd be right back the next week. I was also mindful of the cameras in the room and realized that if anyone wanted to watch and possibly hear what I had to say over in the sergeant's office, they could certainly do so.

I continued to pack my bags and added, "The difference between you and me is that if these guys want to try to push me around, I can push back. You guys obviously can't."

My bags were packed, and some of the guys had started

filing out of G Dorm. The turn of events had been sudden and unexpected, and I wasn't sure what was going to happen next. I'd never been a quitter and had no plans to leave the college without an instructor for an incomplete class. I felt like I owed it to the guys who'd put forth the effort to finish the class with them. I knew they wouldn't get their certificates otherwise, and the certificates meant a lot to some of them.

As I turned to leave, Arthur, who sat right in front of my table, said, "Maybe you won't do this here anymore, but you need to do it somewhere."

That came as a nice surprise. Arthur had a lot going for him but, for the most part, had sat silently through this class. Cole stood and thanked me again for the book. As I was heading to the door, Jeremy stepped in my path with a big smile.

"I'm going to look you up when I get out of here," he said with a big grin. "I appreciate all you did for me."

Arthur and Jeremy seemed to think it would be my last class in the prison, and I'd learned that the inmates were much better at predicting what was going to happen in that environment than I was.

"I'm going to hold you to that, Jeremy," I said. "You gave me the encouragement I needed when I needed it, and I really want to thank you for that."

Jeremy gave me a quick hug and a knowing look. Everyone else had cleared out of G Dorm except my old friend Levi, who stayed in his seat at the table right in front of the far TV.

He gave me one of his big grins and said, "Hey, Mr. Moose." His smile turned into an openmouthed laugh as he continued. "Turns out, they're crooks just like us."

I quickly joined Levi in some much-needed laughter. He waved and stole the parting line I'd used on my students since day one.

"Be good, Mr. Moose."

I walked down the concrete ramp of G Dorm, making a

quick path toward the tiny guardhouse. Some of my students were on the adjacent basketball court, not sure what to do with the unexpected time they were given that morning due to the early dismissal. It was about 8:30 a.m., and the rest of the yard was empty except for one middle-aged man I didn't recognize.

As I approached the front gate and was about to exit into the guardhouse, he hurried within earshot and yelled, "Hey, Mr. Moose, you comin' back, right?"

I turned, lowered my book bags, and shrugged. "We'll see."

The guard who escorted me from my classroom was sitting at his desk in the guardhouse when I came through.

"No hard feelings," I told him. "You're just doing your job, and I understand that."

He responded professionally, "Sorry for the inconvenience."

I got into my car and headed home, the prison in my rear-view mirror. I drove the hour-long trip back to Charlotte, silently sorting out what had happened and what my next move would be. I'd been looking for a graceful way out of the job. The hours were too long—my entire weekends were tied up preparing for the class—and I felt like I'd done everything I'd set out to do. No way was I going to leave my current students without an instructor, though. I had every intention to complete the class I'd agreed to teach, but I resolved on my drive back to Charlotte that the situation was going to, at the very least, bring me closer to my resignation.

A week passed, and Richard returned from his cruise. He worked hard to get me the credentials I needed, but it turned out Mr. Clean never started the paperwork, and it was going to be a lengthy process that would go well past the graduation date of the current class. Richard had worked in the prison for a long time and had the proper credentials, so he was able to continue his part of the class Mondays through Wednesdays.

I thought about it over the upcoming weekend and decided

that was it for me. I'd been offered a graceful way out of my prison teaching experience, and I was going to take it. I would hopefully someday teach in prison again, but it would be with some parameters. I would want the opportunity to interview prospective students and would cut the classroom hours from half a day down to no more than an hour and a half.

I wrote a quick email of thanks to Sarah along with a note of my immediate resignation. She had faith in my ability to teach when no one else did, and I could tell she believed in what the college was doing at the prison. I reminded her about the guys at the locker plant who were on work release thanks to her and the few who had been hired permanently.

"Your hiring me changed some lives for the better, and I hope you feel really good about that," I wrote to her in my final email. I meant every word.

I was sure the prison community was all abuzz about Mr. Moose's unexpected departure, and I got a call from Ali the following week. When an inmate called from prison, there was a process by which the receiver of the call could accept or reject it via a recorded message. The phone Ali was calling from was located in the dayroom in G Dorm. I'd spent hundreds of hours in there, and I knew exactly where he was standing. Even though I'd only been gone from the prison camp for a few weeks, it felt like Ali was far away. At that moment, I knew I would never be back.

"You did the right thing, Moose," Ali said.

"No hard feelings toward anyone," I told him. "It was an opportunity to make a clean break, and I took it. I hate that I didn't get to finish my class or say goodbye to you or any of the other guys, but that's sort of fitting. That's how it usually goes in prison: there one day and gone unexpectedly the next."

I spent the next weekend cleaning out my book bags and boxing up my class material with mixed emotions. My good days teaching had been extremely rewarding, and even the bad days weren't all that bad. I'd fulfilled a long-held dream to teach and met some extremely interesting people along the way. As much as I tried to teach what I knew to the guys I met there, I realized that what I told my first class on my first day as a teacher held true—I learned a lot more from them than they could've possibly learned from me.

My newfound free time was spent at my locker business. My nephew had it running full steam at that time, and I felt like I was needed there more than anywhere else. My parents were both in their early eighties and going through some of the typical problems people of that age experience, so I planned on spending my available time with them as much as possible.

I'd needed a break from teaching anyway.

CHAPTER FIFTEEN

My Final Day as a Drug Dealer

"Remember that life's greatest lessons are usually learned at the worst times and from the worst mistakes." —Unknown

WHENEVER I DISCUSSED MY PRISON teaching job, I typically got one of two reactions: "God bless you" or "Why are you wasting your time?" The responses seemed to hinge on whether that person regarded prisoners either as people who had made mistakes and needed guidance or dangerous people who couldn't be helped—I could appreciate both perspectives. Once I was inside the fence and got to know some of the incarcerated men, I realized I wasn't much different from a lot of them. I was just luckier.

I will never fully understand why I wasn't arrested that night in the restaurant more than thirty-five years ago. But there were no cops waiting for me at my car when I left after my manager's threats. I drove home slowly, scanning the rearview mirror for the blue lights I was sure would soon be lighting up behind me. Despite my raging paranoia, nothing seemed unusual. I drove the most circuitous route I could think of to get home. No one followed.

I'll never know if my partner's greed is what saved me, pure dumb luck, or God himself, but I became a changed man after that experience. I returned the half-pound of marijuana to my accomplice and announced my immediate retirement from the illegal drug trade. Had I been arrested like I expected, I wouldn't have completed college. I doubt seriously that my father would've wanted me to work at his business after my incarceration. I wouldn't have married the woman I did and wouldn't live in the house I live in now. I certainly would've been in prison, but not as an instructor. Maybe the opportunity to teach inmates was my penance, my way of paying back the grace that was bestowed on me. If so, I'm thankful for that opportunity.

Even years later with the benefit of hindsight, my prison teaching experience still seems surreal. I was given the opportunity to spend time in a world rarely seen by people who are not, in some way, directly involved in the penal system. My goal in writing this book was to take the reader with me through the prison gate and provide a personal account of what I experienced. Everyone is free to draw their own conclusions as to whether it's worth our time as a society to provide resources to the multitudes of imprisoned people in the United States who want to improve their lives, but my perspective became clear after spending some time with the incarcerated.

Entrepreneurs by nature are generally people who don't like to follow rules. In order to be successful, they have to find a different way of delivering value to their marketplace, and this requires developing unique perspectives and throwing the old rulebook out the window. The entrepreneurial way of thinking can lead to rich rewards, but it can also lead to a prison sentence, especially when the rule breaker is new to the game and figuring things out. I stand as a prime example of that. Our prisons hold a substantial population of entrepreneurial talent. From the small sample size I encountered, I met quite a few men who made an early mistake in life, learned from it, and were ready to make the remainder of their lives worthwhile. What held them back was the lack of information available in their environment.

I got to know many able-bodied, intelligent, incarcerated men who were denied the resources they needed to prepare themselves for a crime-free life upon their release. Not only are these people set free into a world for which they have not been prepared, they also leave prison with a permanent blemish on their record that makes obtaining even the most rudimentary job challenging. I found it to be a complete waste of human potential. The problem can be remedied if we provide those who are ready to make positive life changes with the resources they need to improve their chances of leading a successful life upon release. I believe it's in everyone's best interest to invest in the incarcerated who are ready to become productive members of our society.

I experienced only a small part of how one minimum-security prison operates, but I saw enough to draw some conclusions on what works and what I believe could be improved. I believe prisons exist for a good reason. They not only provide a time-out for people who need to rethink some of the decisions and actions that put them there but also provide a deterrent for those who would otherwise unreservedly break the law. In my time there, I had more than one inmate tell me they needed their time in prison to discover the root causes of why they were locked up.

Although I understand the necessity of a prison system and the importance of making it an undesirable destination, the strategy to make the experience solely about punishment is a poorly designed plan. The minimum-security prison I taught in was likely typical of many, and time spent there as a ward of the state appeared to be an unpleasant experience. Inmates spend years away from their families and the people they care about. They're not permanently assigned their own clothes. The underwear a guy wears one week was worn by someone else the week before. Food is limited and monotonous, and the sleeping quarters are small common rooms lined with tiny metal bunk beds where one loud snorer can make sleep impossible.

The best thing that can happen to an inmate at this level is that they'll someday be assigned a work release job to work third shift in a local factory for a meager wage. Sentencing someone to spend years in that environment with no reprieve seems like punishment enough to me. I believe that the discomforts of prison life, even in a minimum-security setting, provide a suitable level of punishment and deterrence to make the system effective. Inmates are deprived of all the creature comforts people on the outside are accustomed to, which is how it should be. Prisons should continue to make it policy to deny their residents certain amenities.

To deprive incarcerated people who are ready to put prison behind them the necessary resources to make positive changes in their lives makes no sense to me at all, however. Part of the incarceration procedure should include a screening process that separates the motivated individuals who are ready to move forward upon their release from those who have accepted the cyclical prison experience as a permanent part of their life. The motivated inmates would be provided with access to a variety of relevant information designed to assist them when their release date arrives and they rejoin free society.

Learning how to function as a productive member of society requires access to information that is typically unavailable to American prisoners. Electronic devices are prohibited, use of the internet is banned, and the libraries have a limited supply of current information. If an inmate grows weary of the prison lifestyle and makes the decision to improve themselves—and has the determination to do so—they're still woefully behind. My teaching took place between 2017 and 2019, and I had students who'd never been on the internet, never sent an email, and never heard of Netflix. There were days when I was met at the gate on my way into the prison by an inmate who wanted me to look something up, surrounded at break by guys who all needed information on a variety of topics, and followed to the gate on my exit by a different inmate asking me to research something. The constant attention was initially flattering, but soon became exhausting. I realized early that I was basically the only source of information at their disposal.

Before my teaching experience, what I knew about prison was what I'd seen on TV: everyone was a crazed killer wearing an orange jumpsuit and shackles and constantly looking for an opportunity to escape. As I became more familiar with the surroundings, I realized that many of the men there were guys who'd grown up in desolate environments—guys who either hadn't been given opportunities for education or failed to take advantage of what was offered. Many grew up without positive role models and had made bad decisions, leading to the crimes which landed them in prison. Not *all* the incarcerated are victims of their environment, but put me in some of the places they came from, and I could see myself making the same poor choices.

The principles of the people who raise you naturally have a strong influence on shaping your values when you're young. I was fortunate my father sold lockers and not cocaine. When I was growing up, he talked about the good salesmen he managed and some of the great deals they'd made for his company. Those high-achieving salesmen had my father's respect and admiration, so naturally, I wanted to be just like them. Similarly, the high achievers who grow up in low-income environments are often naturally drawn to the people who appear to have found a way to break the poverty cycle. In this setting, these are often drug dealers and other types of lawbreakers. Their criminal lifestyles appeal to the motivated and business-minded who aren't provided with legally viable choices.

The guys I got to know in the minimum-security setting got to the honor camp I worked at by staying out of trouble and playing by the rules. Some of those I met were in prison for their second or third stint, and some were there because they'd experienced one bad night. After a short period of time, it was fairly easy for me to recognize the guys who'd accepted cyclical returns to prison as a permanent part of their future and the ones who'd made the decision to never return. Yet the prison system is designed to treat all inmates the same and provide them with the same experience and lack of resources.

The prison system can cause an inmate to lose their sense of identity. Dehumanizing them makes it much easier for the people in positions of power to do their job without the temptation of showing favoritism to anyone or getting too affable with someone. Upon entry, an incoming prisoner is given the same uniform everyone else wears and is assigned a number. This number becomes a big part of their new identity, as they're usually referred to by the prison number they were assigned, their last name, or a nickname. My practice of calling students by their first names likely went a long way toward making them feel like an individual instead of a faceless cog in the big wheel of the criminal justice machine.

Along with the common loss of self-identity, I heard the same story time and time again from many students and guys I met inside the fence.

"I was feeding an addiction at the time and was making terrible decisions."

Studies have shown that 21 percent of state prisoners committed their crimes to buy drugs, and 40 percent were under the influence when they perpetrated their crime.[5] Should the offenders who were feeding an addiction be treated the same as premeditated violent offenders?

Although starting a small business is a great option for someone with a felony on their record, I realized early in my teaching experience that entrepreneurship was going to be a great challenge for many of my students. Not everyone has the desire or ability to run their own business, and starting and keeping one running properly is one of the most difficult challenges anyone can attempt. Everyone has a relationship with money, though. With the extra time afforded to me by the college, I spent three weeks of my classes on personal finance. These were the classes that would consistently bring guys in from the yard. One day, I counted eighteen people crowded in the small, humid dayroom who were there to learn about real estate investing and IRAs.

I can think of no greater cause than to teach financial literacy in a prison setting. The connection between growing up poor and becoming a denizen in the US prison system is clear. Boys who were raised in families whose yearly income was in the bottom 10 percent are twenty times more likely to spend time in prison in their early thirties than those raised in top-earning families.[6] This might explain why more than 60 percent of the incarcerated are there for money-related reasons.[7]

Many of my students had no grasp of the most basic financial concepts, such as earning interest on an investment or how a debit card works. The topic of money held their attention more than anything else I taught. Many had likely never been exposed to this type of information and were eager to learn. I believe that teaching soon-to-be-released inmates the basics of financial literacy is one of the clearest steps we can take to reduce the recidivism rate.

Can we help them all? No. Only those who are ready, willing, and able to make positive changes in their lives. When people asked me what it was like to teach in prison, I often said it was like throwing a lifeline to a drowning man, with the difference being the man usually didn't know he was drowning. All I could do was throw my rope out there and try to pull him to the shore for a different and more prosperous life. But I couldn't do anything if he didn't grab the rope.

Based on my time behind the fence, I know I can structure a program that could help hundreds, if not thousands, of incarcerated men and women break free from the prison cycle. Even if the sum of my efforts results in helping only a handful of people turn their lives around, it's a worthy endeavor because it also improves the lives of the generations that follow. The most rewarding occurrence in my time teaching was helping someone gradually realize they had options other than spending the remainder of their lives going in and out of prison. It didn't happen often, but when someone unexpectedly grabbed the rope, it made up for all the difficult days, and then some.

I want to thank you for reading this book and helping my cause. I also want to ask you to think back to a mistake you might've made at some point in your life that could've put you in the same situation I was so fortunate to avoid. Have you ever driven after having too many alcoholic drinks? Taken something that didn't belong to you? Or, like me, got caught up in an illegal business? One mistake is all it takes for someone to dramatically corrode their life forever, and the dehumanization prevalent in the punishment system yields few resources to its denizens and little encouragement to earn a second chance.

I came close to becoming an inmate in the North Carolina Correctional System at a young age and living the rest of my life with the burdens from a felony. I was young and thought I was completely invincible. I'm a different person at fifty-eight than I was when I was taking those reckless chances at twenty-one, but my independent and non-conformist spirit is still there. It's there in many inmates, too.

The closest most people get to a prison is when they drive by one. If you pass by at the right time on a nice day, you might see the inmates in the exercise yard lifting weights, playing basketball, or sitting at picnic tables, all wearing their matching prison uniforms. The prison system by design makes them all look identical.

What I learned by spending time in a prison is that, although the vantage point is much closer on the inside, the conclusion is the same. If you adjust for different upbringings, different role models, and different twists of fate, they're all about the same. All about the same as you and me.

Epilogue

"When education and resources are available to all without a price tag, there will be no limit to the human potential."

—Jacque Fresco, American futurist and social engineer

I WAS UNABLE TO LOCATE many of the men I met during my stint as an instructor, but this is a progress report on a few:

Ali:

- Began working for my company June 8, 2020
- Quickly promoted to operations manager
- Managing several successful construction ventures

Anthony Williams:

- Author of *Clerical Mistake* and *Clerical Mistake II*
- Founder of a successful chauffeur service in New York City
- Founder/operator of a successful medical transport business

Benny:

- Founder of a successful courier business

Cameron:

- Founder of a successful painting company

Clayton:

- Founder of a successful nonprofit rehabilitation organization

Josh Proby:

- Author of *The 30-Day Journey from Prison to Spiritual Peace*
- Founder of a successful clothing line
- Successful motivational speaker
- Founder of a successful trucking company
- Founder and operator of Peace4Poverty, an organization that provides inmates with the education and resources they need to repair their credit and start businesses upon their release (www.peace4poverty.org)

Kendal Williamson:

- Transforming his Idlewood estate per his plans
- Selling mulch and vegetables and converting his dairy barn to affordable housing units
- Served as a minister for Marcus's wedding shortly after his release

Patrick:

- Running a successful general contractor business

APPENDIX:

Logos from Some of My Student's Business Plans

J&K FLOORING & CLEANING
Carpet Installation
Business Cleaning

All About Trucking

SPLIT PRO SHOP HAPPENS

UP
Utopian Pleasures
Beauty, Spa, & Fitness Center

DT
Dunlap Transportation Group, LLC

Landscaping & Power Washing

Mack'nifiteents

BBS

Nate's Electrical

SUNERGY

IMPECCABLE BUILDER, LLC

Sporting World Authority

INK Studios/Komics

BEAUTIFY
beauty salon

Notes

1 Patel, Neil, "90% of Startups Fail: Here's what you need to know. Forbes, 16 January 2015. (https://www.forbes.com/sites/neilpatel/2015/01/16/90-of-startups-will-fail-heres-what-you-need-to-know-about-the-10/?sh=26c558296679)

2 Taulbert, C. L., & Schoeniger, G. (2010). *Who owns the ice house? Eight life lessons from an unlikely entrepreneur.*

3 "Trends in U.S. Corrections," The Sentencing Project, August 2020, https://sentencingproject.org/wp-content/uploads/2016/01/Trends-in-US-Corrections.pdf.

4 Clinton M. McCoy, The Reverse Effect (Clinton M. McCoy, 2015)

5 Wendy Sawyer, "BJS Report: Drug Abuse and Addiction at the Root of 21% of Crimes," Prison Policy Initiative, June 28, 2017, https://www.prisonpolicy.org/blog/2017/06/28/drugs/.

6 Adam Looney and Nicholas Turner, "Work and Opportunity before and after Incarceration," Brookings, March 14, 2018, https://www.brookings.edu/research/work-and-opportunity-before-and-after-incarceration/.

7 "Federal Bureau of Prisons Statistics / Inmate Offenses". May 8, 2021, https://www.bop.gov/about/statistics/statistics_inmate_offenses.jsp

Bibliography

Federal Bureau of Prisons Statistics. (2021, May 8). Retrieved from https://www.bop.gov/about/statistics/statistics_inmate_offenses.jsp

Hughes, Timothy, and Doris James Wilson. "Reentry Trends in the United States." Bureau of Justice Statistics (BJS), 2020. https://www.bjs.gov/content/reentry/reentry.cfm.

Looney, Adam, and Nicholas Turner. "Work and Opportunity before and after Incarceration." Brookings, March 14, 2018. https://www.brookings.edu/research/work-and-opportunity-before-and-after-incarceration/.

McCoy, Clinton M. "The Reverse Effect." Clinton M. McCoy, 2015.

Patel, Neil. "90% of Startups Fail: Here's what you Need to Know." Forbes. January 16, 2015. (https://www.forbes.com/sites/neilpatel/2015/01/16/90-of-startups-will-fail-heres-what-you-need-to-know-about-the-10/?sh=26c558296679)

Sawyer, Wendy. "BJS Report: Drug Abuse and Addiction at the Root of 21% of Crimes." Prison Policy Initiative, June 28, 2017. https://www.prisonpolicy.org/blog/2017/06/28/drugs/.

Taulbert, Clifton and Schoeniger, Gary. (2010) Who Owns the Icehouse? Eight life lessons from an unlikely entrepreneur

"Trends in U.S. Corrections." The Sentencing Project, August 2020. https://sentencingproject.org/wp-content/uploads/2016/01/Trends-in-US-Corrections.pdf.

Acknowledgments

WHEN I DECIDED TO WRITE this book, I wanted to make it the best I possibly could. I would like to genuinely thank everyone who helped me make that happen:

Reba McLaughlin—My amazing wife who has supported all my crazy endeavors and has always believed in me, even at the times I did not believe in myself. Thank you for your love and support and for sharing this amazing journey. I truly love you.

Myrnie McLaughlin—A truly talented gardener who planted a seed by challenging me to write this story. Thank you for your early encouragement and for all your help along the way.

Brad Norman—A brilliant and amazing editor who shaped my thoughts and words like a sculptor would clay to make this story flow. Thank you for working your magic!

John H. McLaughlin—A tremendous role model for me personally and in the ways of business. Thank you for your guidance and for showing me how to focus on what's important in life.

Kurt Fleshman—For giving me a lifetime's worth of personal and business guidance and support. Thank you for making me a better and much stronger person than I could have ever been on my own.

C.J. Norman—For providing me with the time away from the office I needed to learn to teach.

Omar (Ali) Markabi—For your vision and friendship. We have helped each other go a long way in a short time.

Tavares James—For allowing me to be a part of Lifeline Education Connection and for providing me with the opportunity to teach again. Our journey is just beginning. www.lifelinetoasoul.com

Steve Parker—For enjoying my early manuscript enough to read it twice. It was the perfect amount of encouragement exactly when I needed it.

David Wogahn—Of AuthorImprints: for your guidance and talents in creating the cover and designing the interior of this book. Thank you for your direction and patience.

Jessica Norman—For another amazing website: www.lifelinetoasoul.com.

Reverend Jim White Senior Pastor at Mecklenburg Community Church—For decades of exceptional spiritual guidance.

Cheryl Sprowl—For your direction as my first reader.

Jessica and Chrissy from Write My Wrongs—For the amazing job with edits big and small.

Peter LoPinto—For your amazing talents and assistance crafting the audiobook.

For the incarcerated men I encountered during my teaching experience who got out and did something positive with their lives. Congratulations! You passed my class.

About the Author

JOHN McLAUGHLIN spent half his life bootstrapping his start-up business to an industry leader. His desire to teach what he spent his career learning led him on a remarkable journey through the gates of a minimum-security prison where he taught entrepreneurship for almost three years. John has an MBA, a teaching certificate, and a marketing management certificate from Harvard Extension University.

John enjoys riding a tandem bicycle with his wonderful wife, Reba, on the greenways of Charlotte, North Carolina, where they live with two extremely spoiled cats, Moe and Joe.

You can learn more about John's current teaching program at: https://www.lifelinetoasoul.com/.

CPSIA information can be obtained
at www.ICGtesting.com
Printed in the USA
BVHW080927010323
659313BV00001B/9

9 798986 689104